CATCHING CHIMERA

THE 21ST CENTURY PERFORMANCE MANAGEMENT

TRIPLE M

(MURARI MADHAB MISHRA)

Copyright © 2024 Murari Madhab Mishra

All Rights Reserved.

This is a work of fiction. All characters, places, events, incidents, and the plot are products of the author's imagination or are used fictitiously. Any resemblance to actual persons, or events, or locales is entirely coincidental and not intended by the author.

The copyright and the rights of translation in any language are reserved by the author. No part, paragraph, passage, text, table, graphs or art work of this book may be reproduced, transmitted, stored or utilized, in original or by translation, in any form, or by any means, electronic, mechanical, photocopying, recording or by any information, storage, and retrieval system, except with the express and prior permission in writing from the author.

Cover Illustration: Omkar U S

First published in 2024

मूकं करोति वाचालं पङ्गुं लङ्घयते गिरिम् ।

यत्कृपा तमहं वन्दे परमानन्द माधवम् ॥

(O Lord, I pray for your grace; for it is with your grace, even the dumb can become eloquent and the lame can cross mighty mountains).

INTRODUCTION

The 21st century world is transitioning into the Industrial Revolution (IR) 5.0 driven by virtual reality and artificial intelligence. While these changes are revolutionizing human performance and productivity, the system used to manage this performance in the workplaces continues from IR2.0, a relic from an era long gone. The fact that it is out of sync with the current reality has been proven time, and again when organizations have discarded performance measurement altogether due to poor results.

Here is an introduction to a new 'performance management system' fit for the 21st century. This is perhaps the idea whose time has come.

The concept has been dealt with, one aspect at a time, in a storytelling fashion to endear itself to the readers, users and decision-makers alike. It is believed that the new system will take root across productive endeavours to make management of performance scientific, contemporaneous, and trustworthy, again.

CHIMERA (GREEK MYTHOLOGY)

The 'Chimera' was a mythical animal made up of a lion, a goat, a dragon, and a snake that breathed fire. She was supposed to be of divine descent but was feared by people for killing livestock and wreaking havoc on the lands of Lycia, it inhabited. The king of Lycia ordered Hipponous (Horse-knower), a contemporary knight, to confront and slay this creature.

The king was not very optimistic, for Hipponous was no match for Chimera. But Hipponous had Pegasus, the winged horse. With the blessings from the gods, Hipponous flew on Pegasus, fought a withering battle with Chimera and slayed it at the end.

PROLOGUE

Maddy, the Head of HR, was pensive. "No one seems to like the current performance management system, professor", she said. "The employees disagree with their ratings. They believe that their manager does not remember all their hard work through the year. The managers grumble that employees do not recall the frequent feedback they give throughout the year. None like the 'bell curve'. And the leadership does not trust the process itself to deliver business results. Is there any solution, professor? Are we destined to fight this multi-headed 'Chimera' endlessly with no victory in sight?"

The professor was more optimistic. "We are students, Maddy. Students of logic, and human failings, rationality, and irrationality, mathematics, and statistics, exact sciences as well as probability. We haven't found a solution only because we haven't looked in the right places, perhaps. Let's disaggregate, declutter, solve, and then reaggregate. Let us deal with this, one step at a time". And thus, the knight and her guide started exploring the contours of this modern 'Chimera'.

CONTENTS

PART I: THE KNIGHT

The Beginning	1
Blue Ocean	4
Journey To The Centre Of Chaos	8

PART II: THE ARENA

Light, Camera, Action !	13
House Of Mirrors	15
Shifting Sands	17
Driftwood	20
Hunger Games	22
Falling On Deaf Ears	26
Lion Vs. Tiger	29
Dance Of The Elephant	33
AWOL	35
Pressure Cooker	37
Crescendo	39
Rear View	41
The Bank Run	46

PART III: THE QUEST

Time Out ! Back To Basics	53
It All Began, Here !	56
Avatar 2.0	61
The Dance Of Demand-Supply	67
What's The Problem	72
Does My Soldier Know What My General Wants ?	76
Zeigarnik Effect	80

Fill it, Shut it, Record it !	82
Psychology Of Free Advice	86
What's In A Name ?	92
Likert Calling	94
Bell The Likert	99
The Psychology of Zero	102
Lost & (Not) Found	104
Hotel California !	110
Attention ! (Bell) Curve Ahead !	113
Swing The Bell	116
Boss Proposes, Superboss Disposes	122
Boss Is Right !	124
Shawshank (No) Redemption	126
Conditional Probability & The Diagnostics Conundrum	130
Conditional Probability & The Performance Conundrum	135
Live, Die, Repeat	138
PART IV: CHIMERA	
An Idea Whose Time Has Come	145
The New Beginning	156
Win-Win	159
Modus Vivendi	161
PART V: THE EVER AFTER	
Instant Karma	167
Dawn Of Reality	171
The Butterfly Effect	179
Epilogue	183
Acknowledgement	187
About The Author	189

PART I: THE KNIGHT

THE BEGINNING

Maddy was excited. She had just landed the Head of HR role for a start-up. Every soldier dreams of retiring as the chief of the forces s/he belongs to, every politician dreams of retiring as the head of the state of his/her country, and every corporate citizen dreams of retiring as the head of his/her chosen function. For Maddy, she was getting 'the' position reasonably early in her career. It was a start-up, fine; a mid-size workforce, fine; a newly carved out role, okay; nonetheless the position with the impact she desired. It was hers to paint this canvas the best she could. She couldn't have asked for more.

Life was not a straight line for Maddy, growing up in a tier-III town in the backwaters of the corporate world. She was good with numbers. She would crack every logical, analytical test with elan only to make silly mistakes in the finals and lose out on being the topper in her class. She chose to graduate in psychology when all her friends went into engineering. Why? Well, she couldn't recall exactly why but knew she could do anything she set her eye on but didn't know what she wanted. She chose to specialize in statistics because other subjects were full of theory and theory bored her. But she quickly found out she didn't quite like statistics either. That didn't stop her from graduating near the top of her class. When she told her professors that she planned to pursue an MBA, her professors were more relieved than her. One of them even went to the extent of saying that he thought she would be a disaster as a professor had she chosen to pursue research after her master's. He didn't have the heart to say so till she made her intentions public. So much for the vote of confidence!

But what struck her was what she heard her professor of organizational psychology, Professor Sai Nathan, say. He had told Maddy to major in whatever field she liked. He was disappointed when Maddy had chosen statistics and not organizational psychology but told her to follow her heart. Now that Maddy was changing course yet again, he was heard saying, "Maddy will do well in whatever she wants, the only question is, what does Maddy want?" Hearing this, she felt a sense of deja vu. Indeed, what did she want?

When she sat for her MBA entrance exam and landed a seat at one of the premier institutes in the country, she joined without hesitation. First few days at the campus and Maddy already felt like this was 'it'. She felt she had finally found something she liked, loved, and enjoyed while being good at it as well. Life in the institute was a celebration; the course intimidating, class hours crazy, course submissions crazier, submission deadlines 12 o'clock at midnight, cafe timings 24x7 and internet uninterrupted (those were early days of the world wide web). It was exhilarating and tiring all at once. Between early morning dash to the class to dozing off in the back benches to getting thrown out of classes by the professors, scoring C's and D's for the first time in life and feeling absolutely no remorse about it, partying the nights out, appearing in unending surprise quizzes, mingling with some of the sharpest minds in the county, and a wide choice of dudes thanks to the still improving gender ratio, all this was a different world for Maddy. Life was a roller coaster and Maddy was having the ball of her life.

CATCHING CHIMERA

When it came to choosing electives, everyone knew Maddy would choose operations the numbers lady that she was. But like a moth attracted to fire, Maddy chose HR! Why? She told her friends she wouldn't enjoy working with numbers all her life. In HR, she wanted to prove to herself yet again that she was up to the challenge. But all of this couldn't explain what she felt whenever she thought about the decision. For Maddy, the choice was, 'strike off all that you don't like, and whatever that's left on the table must be what you really want'. She would recall her statistics lesson, 'existence of anything can be proven by proving the non-existence of the opposite' (phew!). What you want can be found only when you remove all that you don't want; what remains must be what you desire. Then why did Maddy feel a sense of non-fulfillment every time she pursued this method? If only she knew! Anyway, Maddy could do anything if she set her sights on it, right? So Maddy landed one of the most sought-after jobs on campus from a premier software conglomerate besting 16 of her classmates to it. Maddy had arrived at the 'dog eat dog world' of multi-national corporations.

Meandering through the corporate jungle for 15 years, marrying a fellow colleague, raising a boy and a girl while remaining competitive, seeing husband quit the corporate world, bitten by the start-up bug, seeing him fail financially, watching him return to corporate, few years behind his peers - their peers, and adjusting to the pace of 'Instagram' life had become routine. Then came this offer along to head the HR for a start-up. If only Maddy knew how life would change!

BLUE OCEAN

Bangalore was known as the Garden City in the 70's, the 'retiree's paradise' in the 80's, the IT incubator in the 90's and the IT capital of the world during the 2000's. One would remember Barack Obama talking about the US jobs getting Bangalored during the 2010's. The year was 2021. Covid-19 had ravaged the economies of the world in a 'once in a century' kind of pandemic. Bengaluru was no different. The city had seen an exodus of the techies to home bases, permanent work from homes (WFH), depressed demand for real estate, extreme valuation of tech stocks, and a 15-year-old itch for Maddy to see something other than IT. That's when one of her mentors reached out asking if she was interested in joining a pharmaceutical startup as the head of HR. Maddy jumped at the opportunity.

Maddy joined this new company at the beginning of that year. It was a tough conversation getting her previous manager to agree to relieve her. The Manager was aware of her capability to think systems and build them one process at a time. He was a beneficiary of the new succession planning and talent management structure she had put in place. It was widely being used in the organisation and had already generated 5 million USD savings, a very big amount by value and about 1% of the total revenue. However, she was clear in her mind; she must not overstay her welcome. She had done well in that place and had reached her peak performance last year. Unless she was going to get a larger role, it would be tepid growth from thereon. Hence the move to leave an established role and step into the unknown was done, though not without trepidation. Everyone used to say that she was CHRO material and would be a CHRO one day; yet when the day came, she had butterflies in her stomach. A new chapter in her life was unfolding.

Now about the industry. The medicines made by the pharmaceutical industry are divided largely basis the administration route. There are medicines (called formulations) that are consumed orally like tablets, capsules, solutions, suspensions, powders, etc. Then, there are parenteral formulations that are administered directly in the veins or muscles called injectables. Then there is the back-end business of making those active pharma ingredients (called APIs) that go into all these formulations. A new branch had come up in the last two decades, called biopharmaceuticals. These were bio-engineered proteins made by genetically altered live cell organisms grown in labs and cultured in large tanks so the resultant protein could be useful in treating chronic or genetic disorders for which chemical formulation-based cures had not been successful. Each of these divisions had many sub-divisions of course. The over-the-counter medicines were the least regulated of all and were manufactured by the highest number of players. The competition there was intense and the margins - the thinnest. The drugs that couldn't be given without a prescription from the doctor were more regulated. The difficult-to-make and the even more regulated drugs were the injectable formulations. The biopharmaceuticals were the frontiers of the pharma industry.

Fast forward to the start-up Maddy was joining. By the time they entered the market, it had become highly competitive. The high margins of yesteryears had attracted many more players to this business. Technology had helped reduce some of the challenges of maintaining high levels of sterility. Years of operations had steadily increased the number of employees with the experience of running such operations. These experienced industry leaders were now helping new owners set up new facilities and thereby increase the manufacturing footprint. This helped the market gain depth, making these medicines more accessible, and more affordable to a much larger population, but the profit margins razor thin. The strategy to win in this kind of market had come from a prodigy of a trainee in the portfolio design team. There were some innovative products in the market that were ahead of the curve. He had suggested that these could be the next wave the company could ride on.

An example is apt here. Covid-19 had stretched the paramedic resources as the vaccines could be administered by the trained and certified paramedics only. There were millions of such injections to be administered but the number of paramedics, trained and qualified to do so were not going up overnight. This led to a trade-off. The paramedics were prioritizing vaccines over regular shots people needed for diabetes, or such other chronic ailments. Patients were finding it difficult to get a paramedic to administer their shots. This was strange; drug shortage was intermittently observed, but administrator shortage was a completely new phenomenon.

Now this problem presented itself as an opportunity for innovation. What if the injections could be converted into self-administering auto-injector pens! Auto-injectors are not new devices. The device carries a cartridge with medicine and an outer casing to keep it sterile. The casing has the mechanism to inject the right amount of solution into the blood. A set of custom fit needles completes the kit. The technology comes in when an auto-injector is held to the skin with the visible vein and the button pressed. That's when the mechanism of the pen opens the sterile chamber, and the needle moves forward to puncture the skin up to two millimeters. Next, the contents of the cartridge are released into the bloodstream one dose at a time. All this happens without the need for administration by a qualified paramedic. The search for the vein, loading of the cartridge into the syringe, and the skillful insertion of the needle into the vein, all of this is replaced by technology, thereby making the user carry out self-administration following easy step-by-step instructions. In pharmaceutical parlance, this is called a new drug delivery system, or a platform technology, or a drug-device combination. If the traditional drug can be administered using this innovative device, there could be demand from those waiting for their regular shots. This would be a great way to create a new segment of users where none existed, improve ease of application for existing users and command a premium for the services. All this was great news; however, there was a reason the market did not have these solutions. They were expensive. Remember James Bond administering such a shot to the vein in the neck in the movie 'Casino Royale'. These are top-of-the-shelf products. Making them affordable and manufacturing them in large quantities would need a team of dedicated smart professionals in the cross-functional fields of medicinal chemistry, pharmaceutical kinetics, pharmacodynamics, drug-device combination, packaging development, analytical chemistry, method development, and technology transfer apart from large scale facilities with manufacturing capacity for the new platform and quality professionals to monitor the entire process under aseptic environment. In short, this was a typical new-age cross-functional team with collaboration as the hallmark work ethic.

For Maddy's new organization, it meant all these plus limited resources and an extremely limited time frame (it was a startup, remember!)

JOURNEY TO THE CENTRE OF CHAOS

Maddy started off on a good note. The board of directors met the week after her joining. The CEO introduced her, everyone welcomed her. She met the other CxOs in the leadership team. All seemed cordial and welcomed the newest addition to the team.

She started finding out more about the company and the work that she was tasked with. The company had about 3000 employees working across seven locations, five in India, one in Germany, and one in the USA. Of the five locations in India, one was the R&D centre, three were operating sites and one was the head office. The German plant was acquired from the erstwhile owners who did not find it profitable to continue the operations. The site was supplying to the European local market only. This was not the most optimum plan for running a site from that place and at that cost. The products in its portfolio were already genericized, the margins were getting ever lower and costs were inching ever higher. Something radical had to be done to turn around that place. The other site in the USA was in a better financial shape. The sites in India were by comparison larger by their output and relatively less expensive to operate. The board had decided to get all its sites approved by the regulators from the US, Brazil, the EU, and the UK. This was supposed to support the business grow its revenue footprint and diversify its risk. The investment needed in operating expenses (opex) and capital expenditure (capex) was being worked out by the CFO. What she needed to do was to hire the right people and help them succeed with the right kind of performance management system. She jumped headlong into her work starting with her induction.

Maddy visited one of the operating facilities in India. It was a great experience. For the first time she was entering a manufacturing facility that made such high quality medical preparations catering to a worldwide group of patients. The manufacturing locations were made as per the best practices in manufacturing, called GMP or good manufacturing practices. Recent developments had increased the scope of this requirement, so the GMP was re-branded as cGMP i.e. current GMP. Entry to the facility was through an access control area where she had to declare that she had no lipstick, or mascara, or any other makeup so that their presence would not contaminate the medicines. Then the person in charge of the visit made her wear full-body aprons. Almost immediately she started feeling claustrophobic. Temperatures in the control area being a pleasant 22 degrees centigrade did not help. She was feeling like she was literally inside an oven and being kept under a slow burning flame. She thought to herself if she felt like this in only a few minutes what it must be like to work in this suit for the entire shift of eight hours. These must be some of the most difficult and demanding jobs in the industry. While her thoughts were wandering about, her attention was brought back to the feeder line she heard her guide speak about. The fully automated filling machine was processing the medicinal mixture, water for injection and the empty cartridges to give out fully packed auto-injector pens. Multiple steps like washing, cleaning, sterilizing, filling and finally packing was all being done with robotics arms. She and her guide then moved down to the packing area where she observed the product being packed into cartons and then grouped into shippers and loaded on to tertiary packs. From there, they were to be transported and distributed in the country of their destination, ultimately landing at the counter of a chemist or a druggist or a hospital or a clinic. It was a fascinating journey of a drug prepared in a factory in one part of the world traveling to a user halfway across the world as a ready-to-use medication.

Soon enough for Maddy, it was time to deliver, it was time for action.

PART II: THE ARENA

LIGHT, CAMERA, ACTION!

The stage was set, the business enablers were in place, the investments made, and the initial lot of people hired. Soon, the honeymoon period for Maddy was over. It was the first month of the financial year; time to start performing and delivering the results as per plan. The CEO called Maddy and told her that the board had signed off the scorecard for the company. She and her team needed to cascade the goals down to the team members and sign off targets for the financial year for each of the CXOs, then the leadership team at each site, and lastly the individual employee's scorecards. It was time for goal setting in short. She got down to the task in right earnest. A meeting of all CXOs was called. She gave out the details of the score card, shared it and requested them to come back with their own scorecard drafts. The company's scorecard doubled up as the CEO's scorecard. The meeting wound up with timelines of one week for the CXOs to submit their first draft. Nothing unusual here. Things were working like clockwork. She had a good feeling of 'well begun is half done'.

The score cards came in as per plan. The next phase was the scorecards of the R&D site and operations sites. Once that was signed off with R&D Head, the COO and the CBO, the next phase was launched. Each of the site's leadership was given their boss's scorecard plus their site scorecards. They were asked to prepare their own function's scorecards accordingly. This took the whole of next two weeks. Once the function leaders / site leaders submitted and finalized their scorecards in discussion with their bosses, Maddy was ready to roll it out to the entire population of about 3000 employees. The HR team at each site was tasked with getting this done.

Maddy was blessed to have a strong and capable HR team with her. Each of the locations had a location HR head and one or two HRBPs supporting the HR head. They oversaw the entire employee life cycle from hiring to onboarding to performing to exiting. There was a team each for talent acquisition, learning and development, HR operations, and HRIS. These were housed at the corporate level, directly reporting to the CHRO. With these teams, Maddy had a full stack of HR team members.

This team ensured that the goals were set for each of the 3000 employees within the next four weeks. And in about one and half months the goal setting exercise was completed. Well begun was half done!

HOUSE OF MIRRORS

The goals were set in a record time of 45 days for 3000 employees. In a world of goals being set four-five months into the year or sometimes not set at all, this was very unusual for the site leadership teams. There was a lot of back slapping and congratulatory messages. There was even a mention of this to the board in the quarterly review. While the board was of the opinion that the goals were set a quarter late, it was better late than later. Maddy was motivated, so was her team. It was a good omen.

No sooner than the goals were set, ominous clouds showed up on the horizon, however. The BD team had struck a deal with one of the largest business aggregators in the US in January that year. The deal value translated to about 30 batches per month at one of the operating locations, and a capacity usage of 80%, a neat number. The margin, at 45%, was very good for a B2B transaction. The team had started the supplies in earnest. First two months i.e. February and March had gone as per plan. However, April saw launches by two more players. Now the market was crowded. Almost immediately sales and margins, both dropped. The aggregator raised a reset clause in the agreement for both lower price and lower volume uptake. The clause was there of course, but more as a safety valve, one of the many in a list of standard T&C. It was not expected to be invoked at all in the contract, let alone so early. There was little choice but to revise the forecast downwards.

As the team was absorbing these changes, came the news of a breakdown at another operating site. This site had secured supply contracts from some of the top names in the EU market. The EU business was immune from externalities as health was a state subject in most EU countries. These countries had centralised social security obligations. The supplies were secured through tenders floated by government or state-run hospital network bodies. Once a tender was awarded, it ran its term with supply and pricing commitments kept unchanged for the period of the contract. Companies loved this way of working; it gave them margin visibility and predictable capacity utilisation. However, there was a catch; in the absence of competition, the state was entirely dependent on these supplies for meeting and servicing its patients' needs. Any disruption in supplies meant mayhem in the network hospitals, risking patient well-being. So, the tenders came with heavy penalty clauses for breach of supply commitments. One disruption could wipe out a year's margins for the company, besides being blacklisted from future tenders. There was reputation loss in the marketplace to add.

Well, everyone knew the risks and rewards in this business model and played by the rules. And that's why everyone in the company was worried when the news of the machine breakdown came in. The buffer stock was enough to last a fortnight. If the site were not up and running by then, they were staring at losses despite operations. It was a touch and go situation. It felt like the movie 'Enter the Dragon' where, like Bruce Lee in a room full of mirrors, they were battling the unknown.

SHIFTING SANDS

It was the monthly review of business. The leadership team was present. The CEO and the CFO had just come out of a meeting with the board. The mood was sombre. Without any perfunctory remarks, the CEO landed the subject; their goals were being revised; and it was not something they would have liked.

The previous month was tough. They had faced a breakdown in one of the sites. The site teams and the vendor partners had worked overtime to fix the problem and get the line back on its feet. They were saved from potential loss of business, profits and reputation in the marketplace in the nick of time. It was unexpected but not unheard of. Afterall, if businesses didn't throw surprises, it wouldn't be tough to run businesses. This was a good show of teamwork and time-bound turnaround.

However, the success of handling the internal challenges were not replicable in the external challenges they had faced. The US partner had reduced the business volume unexpectedly. It had its reasons but that was not helping the team find the business it had promised to its investors. The CEO and the CFO had been hard placed to explain how they were planning to make good the shortfall. Before the start of the year, the board had okayed the plan outlay. The team had raised the funds and invested in capacity building. All of that was approved on the back of a promised growth in revenue and profits. With the reduction in business, they were looking at a gaping hole in the P&L. The board wouldn't hear any of it. They demanded the team cover the shortfall by bringing additional business. Some of the upside business was brought into base business to fill this gap. But the upsides were upsides for a reason. Now there was no choice. The team needed to change gears.

Another thing had happened in the meantime. One of the blockbuster product dossiers that had been filed with the drug regulators had come back with a request for further data. A query in dossier filing meant delay in approval. It also meant the revised approval date was contingent on acceptance of the response. These were wheels within wheels. The business projection had taken the sales for the last quarter basis previously expected approval date. Now the last quarter business moved by a quarter and the entire revenue stream from this product for the financial year was lost.

It would be an understatement to say that Maddy and her colleagues were in troubled waters. Their difficulties were getting bigger by the day. After updating about the goings on in the board meeting, the CEO paused and checked for reactions. There was an awkward silence for a few seconds. It was broken by the COO who emphatically stated that he was doing everything in his capacity to ensure the operations were on track. Even though the breakdown was a major scare, it had been averted. Everyone in the room understood he was right. However, whether he meant it or not, it also implied that some other team member was to be held responsible for the current situation. The Head of 'Regulatory Filing' jumped in before anyone else could. He was an expert in the complex documentation process that each regulatory body across the world followed. Process research is tough but it's the regulatory people who convert the entire research into paperwork that eventually gets filed and gets the companies the regulatory nod to sell in the regulator's markets. It requires a special skill to be as elaborate as expected by the regulators. Unfortunately, this has some side effects; the people who do this kind of work, day in and day out become equally elaborate in verbal communication as well, an occupational outcome. The Head of Regulatory was a special case among the specialists, the occupational effect on him had reached hazardous levels.

The moment the Head of Regulatory started his long winding response to the reason they had been asked by the regulators for additional data, everyone went for their coffee or tea or mobile or laptop or whatever, in the absence of the option to leave. The CEO sighed and waited for a suitable gap in the monologue to interject.

It came in 10 minutes. The CEO quickly did what he had to and assured the Head of Regulatory that he would let the experts do their job, but he needed results. With this, he turned his focus to the Head of R&D. The R&D folks had to rework their filing plan and bring some other products ahead of schedule. He concluded by giving the mandate to the Head of R&D and the Head of 'Product Portfolio Selection' to submit a revised plan. The R&D Head was a scientist with keen business sense, a rare combination. What the CEO was asking was anything but simple and she knew it. But this was not the time to bicker. They were slipping behind their targets. Everyone had to chip in with whatever anyone could. She said she will come back. The meeting ended with the CEO asking the CHRO, Maddy, to rework and submit the revised company scorecard in consultation with all other CXOs. The commitment to the board was primarily financial. They were not to be touched. Everything else was open sesame.

As an afterthought, it struck Maddy as very odd that the CBO had not spoken a word throughout the meeting.

DRIFTWOOD

The previous month was a messy one for Maddy. She had to rework the scorecard. The business shortfall created by changes in the US market were to be plugged. Everyone at the review with the CEO had agreed to rework the plan. But corporate meetings were meant to give promises, not to keep them. When Maddy reached out to the COO, he said he would come back once the R&D Head reverted with the revised product filing plan. The R&D Head said that the Head of Portfolio needed to give the product wise projections first and suggest the shortlist basis business potential. The Portfolio Head said he had referred the data to CFO; the CFO was yet to come back with the final list basis margin projections. The CFO said, he couldn't decide till the Procurement Head provided the costing of raw materials and packaging materials. The Procurement Head was waiting for the COO to give the nod for material basis suitability of use in the production line; not all RM/PM could be used in all lines, there were glass vials and there were plastic vials; products had specific input material requirements basis their own drug dossier submission. These were non-negotiable.

With the COO at both ends, things were moving in circles with no outcomes. She did the next best thing, published the revised draft with the details discussed in the review meeting. They were an approximation; the CEO responded with a stinker, and everyone got busy with action. Each CXO came back with their inputs and the revised draft was shared in a week. That was the end of it.

Everyone got back to their work routine. Maddy asked the COO if he was planning to update the sites about the changes. The changes would have an impact on their batch planning, changeover, cleaning validation and such other activities. The COO assured that he had spoken with the site heads and apprised them. "What about site quality heads?", asked Maddy. "Why don't you check with the Quality Head", pat came the reply. The COO was right. These are corporate red lines people do not cross. While the COO and the Quality Head went along really well, it was the business need. They needed each other's support. The batches were not counted as finished till quality gave the clearance. The action items on a quality management system remained open unless the operations stakeholders keyed in the change controls. The quality team got pulled up for the open items overrun. They needed to support each other. Therefore, the camaraderie was limited to professional commitments. Neither would walk the extra mile needed. That being the case, the matter of goal update took up the entire month. It got Maddy thinking, "if we took a month to rework the goals, how much time will we take to rework the work?"

While everyone was seemingly doing their bit, together they were coasting along listlessly. This hardly augured well for the performance of the organization. What could Maddy do to improve the situation? She didn't have ready answers.

HUNGER GAMES

Autumn had arrived in the city. The leaves were turning yellow. The weather was getting cooler. The days were getting shorter. It was a pleasant time of the year. The weather within the organization was anything but pleasant, however.

Business had not moved directionally till the previous month. All the charisma the CEO carried and the convincing that he and the CFO did to the board couldn't carry the day. The review was scathing. Revenue growth was off the target, operating expenses were mounting, manpower cost at 50% of the operating cost was putting a strain on the cash flows, cash cycle was stretching to the levels where working capital needs were being met from long term financing, regulatory approvals were not coming as per projections, supplier payments were being prioritised, spare parts were in shortage and so on and so forth. In all, whatever could go south was going further south. The CEO and the CFO barely made out of the board review in one piece.

What goes around, comes around. When the business review followed, it was the turn of the CXOs to get a taste of the same medicine. The CFO was the first one off the blocks. He said he was tired of defending the operations cost overrun with the board every month. He requested the

CEO to invite the COO to the next board review as well. Let the one responsible take the responsibility. Before the CFO could go any further, the COO interjected, "Are you meaning to say that I do not take responsibility? I am the person in charge of operations. It's the biggest job after that of the CEO's. Do you think the operations happen without me taking ownership?"

It was an open secret that the COO aspired to be a CEO; while he was working diligently towards achieving it, this wasn't a slight he was going to let pass.

Before anyone could come in, the COO spoke again, "You say that the operations cost is getting difficult to justify. Please tell me, what has been the month-on-month increase in my operations cost? Have we started consuming more raw material, have we started a new facility, have I asked for more positions, have I hired more people in operations? What have I done to make the costs go up?". There was palpable tension in the room. And what the COO said next, set the cat among the pigeons.

He said, "While I appreciate the concern shown towards escalating operating costs, the investments were planned and executed before the financial year started. There has been no incremental increase in operating costs in absolute terms. However, they appear to be increasing month-on-month as a percentage of revenue only because revenue has been falling consistently over the months. I have sufficient spare capacity in my sites. A simple maths would be adequate to guess where the shortfall is coming from. We seem to enjoy blaming operations for the costs. I say, look at them as capacities, capacities we built to service our business. Now pray tell me, where's the business?"

There was an unwritten rule in the team, no personal attacks. The COO had just crossed the Rubicon. It was anyone's game now. Maddy remembered the last review and how the CBO had gone through it flying under the radar. The COO had taken the heat then as well. This time, he wasn't going to. All eyes were now on the CBO.

Salesmen and women were not known to be reticent. They were a vivacious, 'gung-ho' bunch of 'can do' guys. They might over promise in speech but in action were well-known to be a careful lot. They would whine away to no end while signing on annual targets citing all sorts of business constraints and market problems. They would fight tooth and nail to sign on the smallest possible increase in yearly targets. But once committed, they would deliver over and above their promise. This was typical 'under promise over deliver' mindset that had been created and was being driven by the incentivisation that industries had hard-coded into commercial functions. The disproportionate incentive payouts that come at every additional percentage achievement over target, had this psychological trait ingrained in these bunch of tough guys. So how did the CBO, a past master at this game, get it so wrong?

The CBO was a suave fellow. He had been through the rough and tumble of corporate sales and marketing. He was a veteran of several large names before landing this job. He wasn't new to corporate sparring. However, the year was indeed brutal in terms of business. New orders were slow to come by. Existing orders were getting short closed. R&D wasn't helping with new filings, regulatory approvals were delayed or stuck in limbo. All in all, it was a tough year even for a seasoned professional like him.

The CBO was playing dead all these months but not anymore. His core competence was in question. The efforts he had put in all these months were not giving results partly due to externalities and partly due to the lack of results with BD, R&D and Regulatory functions. But now was not the time to take refuge in externalities. It would make him look weak. So, he took the only path left. Off he went giving a detailed account of the efforts he and his team had put in generating leads, bringing in clients, signing commercial agreements and generating business value; all these he gave out like bullets leaving a gun. He acknowledged that he had not been able to give enough business to the COO to fill his site capacities. He was not going to take all the blame, however. He ended by saying that those, who were responsible for keeping their end of the bargain to ensure executed agreements were operationalized, should speak on why they hadn't done so. It was a jungle, each trying to beat the others to safety. The Hunger Games had begun.

FALLING ON DEAF EARS

The 'Hunger Games', kicked off in the previous month, had affected everyone. The Head of Regulatory and his team had worked night and day to prepare the right response to the regulatory queries. Regulatory, R&D, site quality and site manufacturing functions had formed 'cross-functional teams' to solve the differences on the spot instead of going through chains of emails.

The site quality heads had travelled to the locations of the customers that had held back their businesses citing deficiencies. They pitched the quality compliance history of the sites along with the business development executives. If the customers had reservations, they were addressed then and there. It was a refreshing change from the routine process of customer quality team raising a query, customer purchase functions forwarding them to the client BD functions, and BD finally forwarding these to company quality functions for appropriate response. The responses of course travelled a similar email journey in the opposite direction. To watch this 'freight train' in each direction winding its way slowly back and forth would look comic to an outsider. In reality, it was a criminal waste of time and resources.

Watching the queries getting resolved at 'bullet train' speed was a refreshing change for the customers' top management. The customer quality departments were also perforce obliged to turnaround quickly when they saw the partner quality teams stationed at their sites and responding with speed. It was a case study of sorts by the end of the month.

The regulatory filings had been updated at the beginning of the month. By the end of the month, the regulatory body updated on their website that they were satisfied with the response and were giving clearance to the launch. Some of the customers who had short closed their orders had reordered post intense on-site work done by the quality and BD team. The subsequent month saw the highest number of batches produced by operations. All the right check boxes were getting ticked. It was an intense, draining, maddening but the most happening month by far that year. Everyone was gung-ho about the future.

The board review went smooth, a first in a long time for the CEO. The business review that followed was a far cry from the last one. There was light banter and exchange of pleasantries among the team. Everyone congratulated each other for the teamwork. The meeting was followed by individual half-yearly reviews of each CXO with the CEO. Going by the feedback, all of them went well. Half-yearly reviews for each site, function and team followed.

There was a cascade of the good reviews at every level. Each of the reviews followed a roughly similar pattern; good feedback on the last month outcome, followed by feedback to improve, basis the poor work done during the first few months, followed by positive sentiments expressed by managers that the employee would learn from the past, avoid the pitfalls of failure and repeat what worked during the remaining part of the year. This was typical 'Sandwich technique' on display. All were pleased with themselves, the managers and the employees for having done their share in ensuring organizational success.

One thing kept nagging Maddy, however. The recent success of the organisation was, more than anything else, the result of some serious last-minute scrambling by the teams. While they had scraped through the half year, how many times could they be as lucky! There was no serious discussion around how to be more consistent in the future. The employees seemed to be in an aura wrap of invincibility thanks to their recent success. All the feedback for improvement seemed given without the emphasis it needed. They had fallen on deaf ears.

LION VS. TIGER

The business had closed in green in the first half of the financial year. Everyone seemed high on success. None seemed to recall the journey of two tough quarters. Things had got almost derailed save for some last-minute teamwork. In came success and out went the learning. As the effect of the success wore off, the jagged edges of reality shone back, sharper than ever before.

The next month started off all staid. The teams had gone back to their default mode of working; back to their pocket boroughs. Years of rewards and punishment patterns had deeply ingrained the 'function' versus 'others' mindset in the organisation. Repeated experiences taught employees that good work was more likely recognised by their own functional bosses and their upline bosses. Missteps, however, would be quickly pointed out by other functions. Even in mistakes, while their own function bosses would pull them up in department meetings, they would defend and protect their own in front of their bosses and cross functional reviews. These lessons over years had created deep functional loyalty among employees.

Loyalty is a good thing to have, perhaps one of the best; but an overdose of loyalty to the function was coming at the cost of results to the company. The organisation was looking like one entity from the outside but had become an unwieldy motley group of small silos on the inside with frequent sparring for the spoils of every victory that came the organization's way. This caused friction at frequent intervals. The next one was one 'conflict of functional interest' away. It came during the start of batch production for a new customer.

The commercial team had worked the markets. There was sufficient demand for the products. They had added more capacity, however; more than what could be filled with the current demand. The CEO was aware of this. Before the start of the FY, the board had discussed a new line of business: pharma as a service. SaaS or 'software as a service' was already an accepted reality. Pharmaceuticals business model was more of 'build, own and operate' kind for a long time. Companies in this domain were best valued when they were vertically integrated. But drugs going off patent were changing the rules of the game forever. Companies could no longer get the high margins that came with exclusive rights to patented drugs; a way of life they were used to.

As more medicines were coming off patent, newer companies were setting shop and supplying these at one tenth of the previous prices. The price drop to the patients in some cases were as high as one hundredth; a race had begun to the bottom of the margin pyramid. The older companies were getting newer drugs to the market to stay ahead of the low-cost game. But the pipeline of new medicines was drying out, forcing these to join the margin game, as well.

This was on the minds of the board members as well. The CEO and the Head of Strategy had pitched this. The board had given a mandate to the CEO: Let's do what we know best but not ignore something that may turn out to be the next big thing. Till we figure this model of 'pharma as a service', let us work on the twin engine of existing products growth and new services infusion at a 60%-40% combination. This would give them an early mover advantage in the new segment. They asked the CEO, what he needed to make this work. He and the CFO had asked for more manufacturing capacity. The existing capacity (previous year) was sufficient for that year business. The new business, however, was high volume, low margin game. They needed the extra capacity for this purpose. The stakes were high. But it was the only bet in town. And they had taken it. Long story short, the additional capacity, put in place before the start of the year, was sitting idle. The services business had not ramped up as expected. How to untie this gordian knot, no one knew.

The COO had enough of explaining the low capacity-utilisation. In one of the meetings, he just said, "don't ask me why I have idle capacity, I only produce what's asked of me. If you give me orders, I am ready to service those orders. But no one seems to know when the next order is coming?" With mirth, he asked the CBO when the orders were coming.

The CBO was an old hand in the established products business. He was clocking the target numbers month on month like a pro. But revenue from this 'Pharma as a Service' was going nowhere. While he understood the new business as well as his old, executing it on the ground was a different ball game. He felt like a premium car salesman selling a car to a hitchhiker. It wasn't working. With every passing month, the gap between plan and actual was getting larger. There was gossip in the company that the CBO 'PhaaS gaya', Hindi for 'getting stuck' in this piece of business strategy. The CBO was a career salesman. He wasn't going to shy away from a joust. He launched himself headlong into the intricacies of the service business. The CBO was onto something. Maddy and others listened attentively.

The CBO repeated, "This new business is a mindset challenge first and a challenging science later. To be successful in this, we have to have a mindset of service, a willingness to understand the customer's need, and provide a solution that meets that need. In all our pre-deal deliberations, we found that major expectations were from site operations and site quality functions, where the customer's batches were to be taken. However, our operations team has been clear that our processes are the gold standard in the pharmaceutical industry. We need not modify anything further. The client can get the best quality products following our processes. This is more like the famous Henry Ford example in cars; 'you can have any colour as long as it's black'. How do you run a service business when you display this 'I know what's best for you' approach? The client gets the vibe that there's no intent to address their needs. No wonder our potential clients are turning down orders at the last moment". That's when Maddy understood why the sales guy was giving a long speech. The target was acquired in advance. The coordinates had been loaded. The missile had taken off from his continent and travelled into space. When it performed the re-entry, the target became clear. As they say, "Revenge is a dish best served cold".

DANCE OF THE ELEPHANT

The sparring between the COO and the CBO was brutal. It was entertaining to watch two skilled warriors, at the peak of their game trying to dislodge the other from their perch. None were giving anything away. Punch for punch, shot for shot, the arguments stretched into a long and riveting discussion.

Whenever the COO argued his case of how he was doing his best, one would think this was unbeatable, only to see the CBO respond with an equally good counter on why the business was being brought to the company's doorstep only to see it get turned away in subsequent months. While there was no clear winner, everyone saw how hopeless it was for the business if they kept working as experts in their areas. Maddy had a name to it, 'SME Syndrome'; 'I did my best in my silo' kind of attitude to business. Teamwork was sorely missing. They were consistently achieving local optima (function results) while missing global optima (business outcomes).

Into this toxic mix, came the next surprise from the Quality Head. As much as he was given to theatrics, this time he announced matter of fact that he would be recommending a pause to manufacturing in a week's time due to some things that needed urgent attention but hadn't received any. The room suddenly went quiet. The COO and the CBO momentarily forgot the heated arguments they were having. All eyes were on the Quality Head.

Usually, the Quality Head enjoyed the attention that came with his antics, but not this time; he was sombre. He tabled a report; it was the internal audit report of one of the sites. The site, a relatively newer one, was designed with the use of the latest technology platforms in each of the respective functions. The quality function used the best 'quality events tracking' platform, the production function used a 'production planning and inventory control' platform that was top-notch in its category, the supply chain function used the latest ERP package, and so on. The internal audit, however, had found instances where production records were not matching with procurement records leading to excess inventory build-up in raw materials that was not immediately needed while leaving some others below 'minimum order quantity' without reordering. The story was similar in production versus quality SOPs (Standard Operating Procedures) leading to a mismatch in written records. This was serious from a regulatory viewpoint. It left the Quality Head with the only thing he could do, stop everything, add/edit/remove what was not syncing, check for sync, and then restart the production.

This recommendation of his, bordered on blackmail to the CEO. The revenue was already on the back foot. If the Quality Head's recommendation were followed, it would be pushed further behind. This needed addressing, sooner than yesterday. Little did they all know the other surprises in store for the company.

AWOL

The proposal by the Quality Head had stirred the hornet's nest. It was the same question on everyone's lips: How can there be so much mismatch in the processes? The company had drawn up the business plan much in advance, the capital expenditure plans were approved in advance, work orders were given in advance, and the systems were procured in advance as well. These were not some 'fly by night' systems that they were talking about. These were expensive, globally acceptable, tailor-made platforms. So where did things go so much off the chart?

Though no one wanted to point fingers this time, especially after the bitter experiences these past months, things emerged naturally as all reports were put on the table. The idea of the revenue mix for the year was drawn up at the board level. To have a revenue mix from products and services was a very sensible and future-ready strategy. The Head of Strategy, a veteran of this line of work for many years, and companies had one of the best reputations in this area. He had made this pitch, and it had resonated very well with the board. Their approval had set the ball rolling leading to all other steps culminating in excess capacity. Now the same strategy had got the company into trouble in the interoperability of systems and processes. To understand the genesis of this state of affairs, the team had to revisit the basics of the industry.

The pharma industry had worked on the 'own products'

model for as long as anyone could remember. The industry had taken extraordinary care to weave all its systems and processes around this ownership. It could be safely said that the systems were not designed without due diligence; they were actively designed to meet this kind of business needs. Having the best-in-class systems in each area not only ensured minimum non-compliances but also helped address the regulatory queries in quick time. As for the interoperability of the systems, it was not a roadblock. The number of products being manufactured at a time in a facility were limited but in large volumes. The products were designed in-house so the process parameters changed, if at all, every few years. Even those changes were induced by regulatory process updates, rather than any in-built parameters of the products. So, every time a change was necessitated, all the functions and departments got together and sorted the documentation updates. It was a manual process, and it suited well to the infrequent change requests in terms of cost and time. This was not the case in a service business. Here every customer had different processes in every function and department. Therefore, what was an unnecessary waste of resources in interoperability, became red hot necessity in the new model.

When the business itself was undergoing changes with service focus being the next phase of growth, it was expected that a thorough check of all the effects it would bring along would be examined. This was as much the responsibility of the team making the strategy as the teams that used it. Then, what was the reason the user functions had not looked into this aspect? Were they not fully aware of the repercussions? No one had the answers. In fact, no one could find the Head of Strategy himself. He would not attend most of the meetings citing conflict of meeting schedule and his absence was not noticed by many. But this time around, it became painfully obvious.

PRESSURE COOKER

There was no time to waste. Three quarters of the year had already passed.

The goals had changed by the month. The first round of changes made by Maddy at the behest of the CEO had hardly been cascaded down by one level when further changes brought in by the next month made the cascade superfluous. By the third round of changes, the CEO also lost interest in cascading it any further below his direct reports. So long as the CFO and others knew what was needed to be done, he could demand results from them. How they, in turn, got this done was a problem he did not need to solve. And once the CEO took the pedal off the engine, the CHRO could not generate enough interest among her colleagues to continue cascading changes in goals.

The changes in product mix had led to some scares along the way. The R&D and regulatory teams had scrambled together and delivered the results on each occasion. Yet the gap in filing was still a cause of concern. The team was slated to receive a regulatory update on a blockbuster molecule next month. All eyes were on the regular's website.

The breakdowns had been addressed as and when they cropped up. There's was a percentage loss of cycle time due to machinery breakdown till now. Under steady state conditions, this was not a big deal, but it was not steady state, so nothing could be taken for granted. The operations team was focused on ensuring no further loss of productivity for any reason whatsoever.

The CBO and the COO had got their act and their teams together. The CEO was explicit that any further business fluctuations due to personal chemistry or lack of it among them was going to cost them both and their teams dearly. That seemed to have done the trick.

And finally, the quality team had worked on mission mode to identify the inter-departmental handover-takeover procedures, incorporated them into change control procedures, and uploaded the training requirement on the mandatory training portal. The progress was a good 75% of the population. However, in quality, till 95% of the population was trained and certified, it was considered non-compliant.

This was an anxious time for everyone, and the pressure was ever-present.

CRESCENDO

The pressure of performance was very high.

Watching people race against time to complete their goals, delayed both by internal and external factors was not a pretty sight. Maddy wished she could go back in time and warn them, so they didn't have to go through these high-stress weeks and months. But that was just wishful thinking. Or was it? Who knew?

The moment finally arrived when the year was at the end. Everyone knew they had done reasonably well, especially in the last quarter. But how good was it? To find that out, they had to wait till the CFO published the signed-off numbers.

***

Both the CEO and CFO had come back from the board meeting. They looked relaxed. All around the table were excited with anticipation. And finally, the CFO announced that they had signed off the company performance for the year at 87% achievement. This sounded low. The room fell silent.

The CEO stepped in. It was a tough year, a roller coaster. It was also the first year of a shift in strategy. 40% of the target was from the new services business, a tall order for the first year. Many things went off balance throughout the year. And yet, the set business delivered close to its target at 58% of the 60% share. The new services business was able to clock in only 29% of the 40% share. An 87% total target versus total achievement in the first year was a decent start. The board was pleased with the outcome only because of the circumstances in which it was achieved. The board had made an exception to the rule that no performance bonus be paid at below 90% performance. They had approved payment of bonus at actual i.e. at 87%. The merit-increase budgets had also been approved.

Everyone heaved a sigh of relief. This was good news indeed. Now they understood why the CEO and the CFO were relaxed. All's well that ended well. However, there was a crease of worry. The board had informed that the exception was applied only because it was the first year of the change in the business mix. They would go back to set limits next year. With existing and new business moving to a 55:45 mix next year this was going to be as tough as it could get.

REAR VIEW

The CEO turned to Maddy. It was time for the annual appraisal.

The business results had come in at 87% achievement of targets. The good news was that the performance bonus was granted as an exception at 87% and not zero. All those who had a performance bonus component could now expect a decent payout. The bad news was that the business results had come in at 87% i.e. the company had not done as expected. Now it was time to identify those responsible for the missed 13%. Those who contributed to the success would get good merit increases. Those who did not would get low or no increases. It was time for the bells to toll.

Maddy inaugurated the annual appraisal process with the announcement of timelines. The self-appraisal was to be done in a week. The L1 manager would then give the annual performance rating to each team member within the next week. All the L1 manager ratings would roll up to the respective L2 managers for validation or reconsideration. A week more was apportioned for this task. At the end of the three weeks, the ratings for all eligible employees would move to HR.

While it looked straight enough, in practice a lot of cajoling was needed at each stage. The self-appraisal was the easiest of them all, partly because people didn't need much prompting to write about themselves - we love our own selves. Most of the self-appraisal ended up being positively skewed. However, the next two stages usually went the other way. The L1 managers were a very reluctant lot when it came to giving written feedback. The same guy who wouldn't think twice before giving a dressing down to his team member would need a lot of prodding and cajoling before giving such feedback for the records. Managers, by design, were a conservative lot on this subject. A good performance would draw a comment like 'it wasn't a bad job at all' or 'keep up the good job'; a bad performance would be more like 'there are areas of improvement you might want to focus on'. These comments were neither here nor there. They added very little value to the employee in letting them understand their performance. Then came the least understood step, the L2 manager's feedback and rating. If an employee was confused about his rating, the L1 manager was more confused about what the L2 manager's rating would be. That would be known only when HR published the final ratings. Many a time the rating given by the L1 manager would be changed at the L2 manager level. Some would discuss this with the L1 manager before doing so, some would do it basis their direct understanding of the work done by the employee. More often the employee would get the rating, and the L1 manager would realize the rating has gone up or down from what s/he had given. If it went up, the L1 manager would do well to take credit. If it went down, the L1 manager would conveniently blame it on the L2 manager saying s/he had given a good rating but the L2 manager changed it unilaterally.

Before we get ahead of ourselves, let's go back to what happened when the L2 manager rating was done; all the ratings moved to HR on the HRIS. Maddy's team collected all the proposed ratings and mapped them out on a continuum, famously known as the 'bell curve'.

Most companies follow a five-point rating scale, with the midpoint being the 'performance as per plan' and two points each extending on either side denoting a little above or below plan performance and a large difference in actual performance versus plan respectively. Maddy's organization followed this model as well. However, most of the companies found it difficult to give the worst rating to any but very few. They constituted about 0-5% of the total. The next worst were usually about 5-10% of the total. The 'at par' performers constituted the majority, usually 60%. The top two ratings brought in the remaining 25-30% of the population. There were no surprises when Maddy received the consolidated ratings.

Many companies, realising the futility of running a five-point rating system that by design displays 'central tendency bias' had moved to a four-point rating system whereby the system perforce broke the 'at par' performers cluster into 2 groups, one just above the midpoint and the rest just below the midpoint. This gave a 10-15% bottom cohort, 35% each of the two middle cohorts, and a 20-15% top cohort. This was not the case here. Maddy and the CEO had signed off the 5-point rating scale and that was that.

Irrespective of the scale, the forced distribution did what it was infamous for; it forced people's rating into one of the four or five cohorts based on the mandatory distribution principles. For those, unfortunate enough to be on the border of two ratings, it was a touch and go. When the percentage distribution of ratings was not as per expectations, which was the case in almost all first passes, HR made the most hated move, it called up the L2 managers to moderate some of the ratings downwards to meet the mandated distribution percentage. Here the L2 managers took a judgement call and moved some of the borderline cases one rating down. These were the ones with altered final ratings at the end of the process. Maddy's team did what was expected.

Once HR confirmed that the adjusted distribution was close to the expected distribution, they were signed off by the CEO and published. It meant the ratings were now final and were shared with employees for their acknowledgement. It was time for some happy moments, some sad and some surprises.

Meanwhile, the team in charge of compensation and benefits benchmarking had worked out a merit increase grid for the year working with internal and external benchmarking data. The result was the 'merit pay increase grid' mirroring the 'rating grid'.

Coming back to the situation at hand, there was no provision for a change in forced distribution percentages during a bad year of performance (or for that matter, a good year). For the five-point scale in use in the organization, the bell curve was signed off at 5%, 10%, 40%, 30% & 15% respectively from bottom to top rating and the attached merit increase was signed off at 4%, 6%, 8%, 9% & 10% for the respective bottom to top rating holders. A cursory look would tell that the rating distribution was top-heavy; almost half the people were getting an above-average rating in a year the organization achieved 87% performance. This anomaly was corrected with a merit increase grid that tapered off while moving up the scale. In effect, it neutralised the top-heavy performance as judged by managers with bottom-heavy percentage merit increases.

The end result was tragic. The inability of the managers to differentiate top performers (by packing the top two ratings with 45% of the population), resulted in all top rating receivers, both genuine and not, receiving a smaller increase in pay. It demotivated the genuine top performers. But what it did to the bottom rating receivers was more tragic than even the top performers.

The company had achieved only 87% of its goals. The year was closed, the clock couldn't be wound back. Now that the company had lost a year, it was ensuring the employees (those deemed responsible for the company's loss) were losing out during the next year.

It was like, 'I (company) lost a year due to you (employee); now I ensure you lose a year as well'. In this game of lose-lose there were no winners. It made Maddy think, 'are we really following the right system?'

THE BANK RUN

The stage was set. The annual ratings had been given by L1 managers, normalized by L2 managers, fit into a bell curve by HR, and signed off by the management. The merit-increase percentages had been connected to each rating by the compensation and benefits team. The new compensation letters were ready for roll out. The finance team had been alerted about the upcoming increase in the salary outflow. It was time to roll out the last leg of the annual performance management system, the last act in the annual waltz of the employees and the organization, viz. annual performance-based feedback and consequence management. It was time for increment, annual bonus payment, promotion, transfer, or lack of any/all. Maddy and her team went out and finished the job.

Then, came the time for wait and watch. Like watching out for a tsunami after an earthquake, the CEO and Maddy waited for the employees to receive the details, take a few days to mull over what had happened and then react.

Some would be happy with what they got. Some would not be happy but not that sad as well. Some would be sorry with their compensation growth but let it pass. And then, there would be that lot who would feel downright angry at the injustice in the compensation increase, the tsunami. Mind you, there is no correlation between the absolute increase in compensation and the mood of the employee. The lowest increment receiver could be happy about it and the highest increment receiver could be the most unhappy. This mood was a result of multiple factors like current compensation vis-à-vis the market - real or perceived, belief in correlation between efforts put in and results (compensation) received, knowledge of increases received by peers with similar (perceived) performance levels and many such factors. However, one underlying current would be common among all reasons - perception of fairness of the performance management system in identifying the employees that have actually performed and distributing the rewards among all employees in an equitable manner.

Perceived fairness and equity, real or not, trumped everything else. Some tragicomic situations would best describe this concept:
• Schadenfreude: An employee would be unhappy at receiving a poor rating / increment but would feel less unhappy on coming to know that a colleague has been treated similarly or worse.
• Reverse Schadenfreude, Envy: An employee would be happy at receiving a good rating / increment only to turn sour on knowing a colleague getting better outcomes with similar effort or worse, better outcomes with lesser effort, made famous by the movie '3 idiots'.

As per Murphy's law, all that could play out, played out in the organization during the weeks following the performance rating and increment discussions. There was a spike in resignations; from those who had offers in hand already. There was a dip in employee productivity for a few weeks due to generally depressed morale within the organization. There was nothing that could be done at this stage. If people were leaving even after receiving a good increment, more money would not help. Then there was the question of equity. Would the organization be willing to pander to those who resigned! That would set off a wrong trend with everyone trying to show an offer to get an additional, out-of-turn hike.

While all of this was playing out, Maddy and the CEO met over coffee to gauge the mood of the organization. He was not happy. He thought they had done a great job in getting the best deal from the board during a difficult year. Despite that, seeing employees show no loyalty hurt him. But what struck a chord in Maddy was what he said next.

He said, "Look Maddy, you have done a decent job in getting a handle on things even though this was your first full year here, a different industry for you and a chaotic year for all of us. However, your HR systems and processes are what they are. They work the same in every industry, have a solution for every possibility, all developed assiduously over years. And yet, they keep churning out sub-par employee experiences year-on-year, specifically in the performance management area.

While I am not an expert here, could you tell me when was the last time someone overhauled this system with an eye on making it more relevant to the present age. Look, I started working about 30 years ago when we were using trunk calls to telephone someone, I bet you won't even know what a trunk call is. Today we have come a long way with smartphones and anytime anywhere videoconferencing. Telegram has been replaced with Instagram. But I am using the same performance management system today that I used in my year of joining, albeit with some incremental improvements like quarterly check-ins or continuous feedback. Performance management is the major cog in the business wheel that actually determines how the business did and who in the business helped achieve what it did. And yet, we are saddled with multiple biases, both human and systemic and keep cribbing about it year after year.

Improvement in mileage in a vehicle is welcome, but its incremental. Changing from fossil fuel to electric was an orbit change, however. There has been no such orbit change in the performance management system, not at least to my knowledge. Is this because you HR folks believe that this is the holy grail, or you haven't just tried anything yet?"

Maddy didn't have a ready response. She mumbled something incoherent and thankfully the CEO moved on to another topic. The thought, however, stayed in Maddy's mind like a seed that refused to die. Long after that meeting, it was still on Maddy's mind. After about a week of internal boxing, Maddy couldn't resist any further. She called up her professor at the university.

PART III: THE QUEST

TIME OUT!
BACK TO BASICS

Professor Sai Nathan was a genial person with premature grey hair. They made his youngish face look wizened. He was much younger during Maddy's graduation days, but the crown of grey was already the hallmark. The running joke on the campus was that the prof. was borne with that grey thatch. Eventually Prof. Sai Nathan came to know of it as well. But then, he would only smile, taking no offense.

All that reservedness didn't deter the prof., however, from taking on the students when it came to the subject. He was known as the 'go to' prof. on the campus. Industrial psychology was his SME area. Frequently, he would be away from campus visiting organizations on invitation and addressing their concerns. The class knew there would be some interesting stories on this conglomerate or that MNC every time the prof came back from such assignments. These case studies made the challenging subject of psychology more lively and less boring (in the student days, everything was boring for Maddy and her friends; it sounded uncool if you said you liked studying; you would be branded as a nerd! Somethings never change, whatever generation you belong to).

Anyway, Maddy had stayed in touch with her professors

throughout her work life. Early on, she figured the benefit of doing so, the benefit of refreshing her studies while at work so she could apply them better. That apart, Maddy liked the happiness of such intermittent contact with her college. It rekindled the college-day memories and made her feel younger. She would shortly find out how valuable this habit would prove to be.

***

Maddy had called up Prof. Sai Nathan and had discussed the goings on. A long weekend was approaching. She had travelled to the campus, intent on encashing on the break the professor would get from regular work. It was selfish of her. But the professor was happy to see her. He knew that Maddy wouldn't have put in that effort if it could have been addressed on a call. He anticipated a problem worth his time and that was all that mattered. They exchanged pleasantries and did some random chitchat. After a while Maddy brought up the subject of last conversation with her CEO. The prof listened to her attentively. Encouraged by his silence, Maddy described her previous year's roller coaster of a journey. She also felt that the performance management process was working barely fine when she had started off fifteen years back. Over the years it had drifted more and more away from the realities of workplace largely because the workplace had moved ahead at a rapid pace embracing digitization, allowing technology to transform things that were previously one-size-fits-all into solutions that could be customized at a large scale. These changes were very interesting at personal levels and revolutionizing at institutional levels. But for some reason, the performance management had resisted attempts at change. It did take on changes, sure. However, the core of the performance management remained the same, goal setting at the beginning of the year, annual performance review at the end of the full year. Anything else like half yearly feedback, quarterly check-ins, continuous dialogues, developmental feedback, anytime feedback etc. acted more like mobile phone skins giving a very interesting and engaging look and feel to the entire process but little else beyond that. The core remained a touchpad handphone. Maddy wanted to know if there was any scope to transform, not just do incremental innovation. Was it possible? Maddy was out of breath.

Prof. Sai Nathan chuckled. He liked Maddy for her feisty nature. She seemed to have retained this quality even after years of corporate life. However, she had asked too many questions in one go to get a response. The professor asked, "What do you want to know, Maddy?" Maddy had a sense of déjà vu. What did she really want? She took a step back, pondered over it for a while, puzzled as to where to start. Finally, she seemed to have zeroed in on her target.

"Okay, tell me prof., how old is the performance management system we use in its current form, minus all the frills? How old is the core, unchanged, unalloyed?"

IT ALL BEGAN, HERE !

The professor took some time to organize his thoughts and started.

"The quest for performance and management thereof did not originate in the ivory towers of the business houses as we see it today. The seeds were sown several millennia ago when groups of humans decided to organize themselves into collectives with the intent of pooling in their individual capacities and multiplying the outcomes through interdependencies.

They collectively evaluated the efforts of the individuals at the end of each day, to see if everyone did his/her job so that together each one was better off than s/he would have been on his/her own. The results were definitely positive as could be seen in the proliferation of hunter-gatherer collectives. Thanks to the collective success, each got some extra time and used it the way s/he wanted. Innovations and discoveries were the product of this extra time resulting in continuous improvement and continuous progress in the work division. This progress helped humans settle down into villages, towns and then cities, city states, kingdoms and finally nations states.

This 'sum of the parts are greater than the whole' concept came to be known as 'division of labour' by 18th century.

All through this journey, however, collectives and later societies found out that the contributions of those tasked with their share of work were not equal. While the majority contributed as expected, some shirked work knowingly, some were not good at the work, some were better than others and some were in the wrong work itself. While the efforts of the collective turning into results or lack of it (like a war won or lost) were there in plain sight, the breakdown of the efforts into individual man/woman level contributions or lack of it (who won the war or who caused the loss) needed a system of evaluation.

The earliest form of this evaluation would lead to abandonment of the weakest, fierce competition among those who remained to prove their worth and evolution of these systems into 'rites of passage' at regular intervals. These were the early days, and the systems were akin to 'survival of the fittest'. Then came the civilizations across China, India and Middle East – North Africa. The Indians developed a system of evaluation by qualified teachers (gurus). This became the 'gurukul' or 'guru' school system. The kings developed an evaluation system to choose their generals through demonstration of skills in mock-combat in front of an audience. Ramayana and Mahabharata are replete with stories of such apprenticeships and tests. The Chinese developed a system of evaluation and selection of officials to run their bureaucracy that eventually came to be known as the selection of 'mandarins', metamorphed from 'Mantri' or 'Minister'. The 'mandarin' selection system became the gold standard, developing into civil services selection system in Japan, Korea and Vietnam. It went global in the 19th century with the British East India Company establishing this system in 1806 to select their officers. Their success led Britain itself to adopt this system in 1855. With the U.S. adopting this system with the Civil

Services Act (Pendleton Act) in 1883, the system had firmly established itself in the world of administrative selection, both old and new.

This selection system, however, was just the entry into a long period of work where periodic evaluation of performance was necessary. On this front, there is patchy evidence though. The 'Artha Shastra' of Vishnu Gupta or Chanakya was notable in outlining the management principles in running a kingdom on a day-to-day basis. The Greeks and the Romans had their evaluation system for consuls by the senate and the Chinese evaluated the performance of the royal family members. However, the most dominant form of assessment continued to be war and its outcome; the original 'perform or perish' evaluation of performance.

With the onset of industrial revolution, the need to evaluate business performance, find factors contributing to its success and those dragging it down became urgent. The modern PMS, therefore, is no older than the industrial revolution itself. It grew with it, co-creating its success, learning from its failures and evolving to cater to its needs. The earliest managers were the textile mill supervisors of the '19th century' England who observed the workers at the textile mills and ensured the mills got their money worth. World War I was the first global force majeure literally forcing participants to evaluate their armies' performance much more frequently than ever before. The U.S. military responded with a ranking system to identify and dismiss poor performers."

On this note, prof. Sai Nathan took a pause and looked at Maddy. Maddy was pensive. Finally, she spoke.

"Has assessment of performance been always this negative. I mean, all I am hearing is 'survival of the fittest', 'perform or perish', 'do or die', 'run faster than the slowest', 'compete to survive'; all this sounds pretty depressing. Did we design the performance management system only to eliminate poor performance! Where is the 'development agenda' in all this! Do we believe performance can improve or it is just an eyewash!"

Prof. Sai Nathan sported a wry smile. "If this behavior has persisted this long, you know it has deeper roots than just what meets the eye, right! You studied 'loss aversion bias' in your graduation days, Maddy, isn't it? What does it say?"

Maddy thought about it and said, "Well, it is an irrational behaviour wherein people are more interested in avoiding losses than in achieving gains". Then the bulb switched on. "I will be damned!" she cried aloud. "The human psyche is quicker to point out a mistake in others than something well done because it is more attuned to loss aversion than gain achievement. Whoa! And I always thought people were weird to complain! But now it makes sense. Why did I not take up this specialization in psychology back then!"

Prof. Sai Nathan smilingly said, "Told you the same back then, but you were hung up on statistics." And they both laughed.

But Maddy was not done. Almost immediately she asked, "If people are loathe to see losses more than they make gains, and are prone to point mistakes in others, how come, they do a U-turn when it's about their own selves?"

The professor was quick to the point. "Yes, you are right. People do not perceive their own selves that critically. This is due to two things. First, the loss and gain are extrinsic to our own selves. When we lose or gain something, it is not a part of us. Now that 'loss aversion bias' does not hold true for intrinsic evaluation; another bias takes over during self-evaluation called 'self-positive bias' or the Pollyanna principle. Moreover, the mind works at the conscious and the sub-conscious level. While at the conscious level, the mind focusses on the negative, at the sub-conscious level, the mind is very optimistic. An interplay of these two factors makes us overestimate our personal achievements while remaining critical of others' achievement."

Maddy did a mock kowtow but was genuinely pleased to have approached the subject matter expert. She was relieved she was receiving the right guidance. The professor on his part was ever obliging for a round of Q&A. Students like Maddy helped him stay sharp.

AVATAR 2.0

Maddy was pleased. Next was the modern performance management system and its origins. If she could reach the source, she hoped she could unlock its secrets. She felt like a PS5 gamer, a knight in search of this multi-headed beast - Chimera and the professor was her guide in her quest.

"So, what are the contours of the modern PMS, Prof.?" asked Maddy. This time, the professor was quick off the block. It was familiar territory.

"Let's start where we had paused, WWI. During WWI, the U.S. introduced performance rating system to better manage the frontlines. In parallel and independent of these efforts, Walter D. Scott of WDScott & Co., a management consulting firm from Sydney, Australia developed a system of evaluating performance of company workers. This too was a graphic rating scale. Some credit Walter with inventing the modern, annual performance appraisal system. However, the system became truly popular during WWII; wars have a way of heightening the need for performance measurement. It was used to identify, promote and fill vacancies in the hierarchy (no points for guessing why the vacancies were coming up).

In 1950, the passing of the 'Performance Rating Act'

into law by the US was a watershed moment in the history of performance management. This was the first time the federal govt. employees were to be mandatorily evaluated for their performance for the year. Based on the outcome of the evaluation, they were to be given one of the three summary ratings, 'Unsatisfactory', 'Satisfactory', or 'Outstanding'. The explicit purposes of the system were 'identification of the best and the weakest employees' and 'improvement of the supervisor-employee relation'.

With this, the 3-point annual performance-rating scale was born which, with its twin the 5-point annual rating scale, has practically stood the test of time till now.

Maddy had never heard of the 1950 Performance Rating Act of the U.S. She was puzzled. "This can't be true, Prof., I recall nothing about this from my MBA days. In fact, we have read of the 1950s to be the decade of Peter Drucker's 'Management by Objectives'. The practicality and ease of implementation led MBO to become the PMS of choice for almost all corporations of that time."

The professor smiled. "Do you know that the US governments, federal and local, employ about 17% or one in every six employees in that country! It is natural that they would have had to grapple with such scale and complexity more than any other employer. From this point of view, it is completely logical and expected that they were the first to put in place a performance evaluation system that was standardized, replicable, and stood the test of fair practices. It is another thing that the governments are not as good at publicizing their work, they just publish these in their 'gazette' notifications. It's the business companies, consulting firms, and management gurus that publicize their work very well. Besides, the govt. is the last place we look to for innovation. That is a probable reason a lot of us missed it". Maddy couldn't agree more.

As an afterthought, the professor added. "If it gives you some satisfaction, by the 1960s almost all top 500 employers in the U.S. had moved to annual performance appraisals with graphic rating scale, popularly known as 'Likert Scale'. That's the true 'proof of the pudding' for you, Maddy".

"But what about MBO then?", persisted Maddy.

"MBO was a process of setting the goals, 'Likert Rating' was the process of recording the outcome. One helped start and run the performance evaluation, the other helped close it at the end of the year. They complement each other, not compete".

"Then why haven't they remained the preferred system of choice for corporations", quipped Maddy.

The professor replied. "They did. In fact, Andy Grove and John Doerr upgraded MBO to OKR at Intel by the 1970s. The OKR became famous and was used by more corporations by the late 1990s and early 2000s. Balanced Scorecard (BSC) was another offshoot of the MBO, pioneered by Kaplan and Norton of Harvard in 1992 by moving from a single measure of performance to a composite score involving MECE principles - mutually exclusive and collectively exhaustive."

Maddy was genuinely impressed. The professor was a storehouse of knowledge. But Maddy was not giving up either. She pressed on. "Fantastic! MBO, OKR, BSC, alone or in tandem should have solved the problem of managing the performance of employees in corporations. Why didn't they?"

The Prof. ruminated over what Maddy had said. Slowly, he started again. "Of course, the systems were a great improvement upon their predecessors. However, they were continuously dependent on external goals. MBO needed objective setting at the corporation level. OKR added Key Results to track. BSC brought in multiple objectives. Each, in itself, was a great improvement. However, the dependency on externality remained. What was logical failed at the altar of human emotions. Employees were people. And for people to perform, placid objectives would quickly become boring targets. There was no competition, no animal instinct to go for the kill. It was like winning against a computer (computers would of course come later), winning against a person was that much more adrenaline pumping, that much more satisfying, and that much easier for a manager to exhort an employee and get results out of (remember wars!). These systems were failing not due to some flaw in them. They were failing because of the mismatch in user needs. Classic case of 'square peg in a round hole'."

Maddy was quick to acknowledge. She recalled the debate between Adi Shankaracharya and Mandana Mishra to find what was superior, the practice of rituals or meditation on the ultimate. She was enjoying every bit of this theo-practical conversation. The task at hand brought her back from her reveries.

The professor continued. "You see, the element of competition was missing in this scheme of things. It was Jack Welch of the GE fame who perfectly exploited this human trait for business performance. He revolutionized the performance management system in the 1980s with his 'forced ranking system' infamously known as the 'bell curve' method. For the next 3 decades (overlapping with competing systems), employees were being measured against each other, along with an external standard. Using this system companies did not have to create absolute benchmarks as required by the MBO kind. The employees, through internal competition of the 'dog eat dog world' fame, were continuously upping the performance bar just to be sure they did not fall in the last 5-10% that the company had decided as the lower cut-off. Those that were left in that bottom category were laid off at the end of the year."

Maddy interjected, "So how different is this from the jungle rule? The deer didn't have to run very fast. They just had to be faster than the slowest among them. The jungle teaches survival, not excellence. How was the corporate world expecting any different?"

Prof. Sai Nathan knew Maddy was right. But now was not the time. Agreeing with her would mean losing the argument; and the prof. was not done yet. He took off again.

"By the 2000s the corporations saw the futility of swinging from one extreme to the other. Employees could not be made to go through the arena like gladiators and come out in one piece, mentally. While the bottom 5-10% were asked to go, no one was sure who was next. This meant even (relatively) good performers were constantly stressed and, on the lookout to jump ship. The pure objectives-based system was also failing as employees were hardly ever going to behave objectively. In 2002, Colorcon, a pharmaceutical dye maker famously ditched the traditional annual reviews. In 2011, Kelly Services became the first big firm to jump ship, rather, jump off the ship. That year, they abandoned the system of annual performance evaluation altogether, replacing it with frequent informal check-ins. Adobe followed in 2012 and by 2016, the likes of Deloitte and PwC had followed suit.

Today the business world is in flux. Many are still stuck in the 1950s-made model of annual performance appraisal using MBO or one of its variants and 3-scale or 5-scale rating; a few have abandoned all this in favor of continuous feedback. While the annual appraisal process did not prove to be useful as expected, abandoning appraisal itself was like 'throwing the baby with the bathwater'. If there is a problem, there has to be a solution, just that we haven't found it yet."

And this is where Prof. Sai Nathan and Maddy decided to call it a day. They promised each other they would continue the discussion the next day.

THE DANCE OF DEMAND-SUPPLY

Maddy was refreshed from a good night's sleep. She couldn't recall when she had a stress-free day like the previous day. She was meeting Prof. Sai Nathan at his residence on campus. It was a weekend and the prof. did not have any engagements. They had coffee together. It was the professor who initiated the discussion.

"Maddy, the journey of performance management through the 1940s till the 2010s was peppered with innovations, improvements, and course corrections. However, you must also have noticed that the process of measuring performance swung frequently between goal measurement and growth measurement i.e. development needs of employees. You had asked me, 'where's the development agenda?' and we didn't take that up yesterday. Tell me, where does that fit in?"

Maddy said, "Hey prof.! I had asked that first. You can't put my question back at me".

The professor smiled. "Fresh day - fresh start; anyway, let's explore. During WWII, it was imperative to find the right soldier. It was around this time that Abraham Maslow came up with the 'Theory of Needs'. Right after the war, there was a decade or so of rapid growth famously known as the 'baby boomers' era'. By the 1960s the societies across the world were out of the colonial era. It was a time of possibilities, a time of strides in techno-scientific areas, a time for hope, and a time to focus on human development. Wars and competing for resources were a thing of the past. Collaboration and focus on each individual and his/her needs were in focus. 1961 was the year David McClelland published his book, 'The Achieving Society', in which he propounded each individual's motivations. It was also the time when a new labour supply was taking off in the developing world. Remember all of them had gotten their freedom in practically the same decade or two. They were making an attempt at building their own nations. So, the wave of immigration from the developing world to the developed world had not taken off by then. Then came the 1970s and the 1980s when the U.S. got off the gold standard, inflation in the developed world shot up, resources became scarce, growth was muted, and the labour supply was increasing every year thanks to the population boom at home in each country and immigration to the developed world. By the 1990s, the developed world population had peaked. The spike in inflation had given way to a slowdown in major economies, the emerging markets were coming up on the horizon. And by the 2000s, the country-wise business composition was shifting back to balance with more and more corporations from emerging markets joining the top 100 by revenue and people size. The IT industry truly took off during this decade, replacing traditional brick-and-mortar corporations as the largest employers across the world.

Now let us look back at the performance management evolution through these same years once again", said the professor.

Maddy was listening with rapt attention. The professor was establishing a correlation between the data he just put on the table with his next set of data points, this was clear.

A statistician would smell correlation from afar. But what was it?

The professor continued. "WWII was a crunch time to find the right soldier, the commander, and the general. 'Potential' was the key. The massive amount of rebuilding that followed post the war demanded strict checks on the execution of the work being executed. Performance was the key in this era of execution of mega projects. That's when the MBO and the rating scale were the need of the hour. If not for Peter Drucker, it would have been someone else but the time for this had arrived.

Then came the 1960s when pure labour input couldn't sustain the pace of techno-scientific advancement. The average education level of employees went up from graduation to post-graduation; more and more specializations were coming up. When this coincided with the shortage of skilled manpower during those times, corporations were forced to pay attention to the developmental needs of the employees. These were the days of 'motivation' and 'development', in other words, the decade was one of 'employee' in focus.

Next came the 1970s and the 1980s of tepid business growth, high inflation, resurgence in employee base in developed nations due to immigration and other factors, eventually leading us back into high-performance focus. If not for Jack Welch, someone else would have taken the initiative to focus on competition and delivery. That time was ripe for that solution.

The 1990s rise of new sectors of employment, powered by technology, was making corporations switch their focus back on employees. 'Balanced Score Cards' made their way into performance evaluation around this time. The population slowdown was sending fewer and fewer incremental new employees into the workforce. Therefore 'development' was back in focus.

The 2000s were more chaotic with the center of gravity moving eastwards and technology-wards. For the first time, giant software corporations were employing white-collar workers in droves. And these employees were not attached to any plant or machinery that could measure their productivity. In fact, the employees themselves were the so-called machines that generated business. This meant these large-scale employers had to keep a sharp eye on both performance and development, performance because the business delivery depended on it, development because these new machines (the people) needed constant upgradation, nothing new there, all machines need it, just that upgradation here meant 'development'."

The professor paused here and asked. "So, what do you make of this, Maddy?"

Maddy thought for a moment and said, "There seems to be a correlation between labour supply and shifts in performance-development focus. Every time the labour is in excess supply, corporations do not need to invest in development, they demand performance. And when the supply is constrained for some reason, they are forced to invest in the development of what they have."

"Attagirl!", cheered the professor, spilling some coffee in the process but he didn't seem to notice.

Maddy continued. "However, the 2000s threw a spanner into this cyclical performance-development flip-flop. Technological advancements coupled with proliferation of new work fields have neutralized the effect of high supply of skilled workforce from the developing world. This made corporations seek performance and development both from the people systems."

And as if on cue, Maddy and the professor together said, "And this is making the existing system flounder". Both laughed at the unplanned, synchronized last sentence.

After a long pause, the professor added, "However abandoning appraisal itself is like 'throwing the baby with the bathwater'. If there is a problem, there has to be a solution, just that we haven't found it yet."

The professor was repeating himself from the previous day. It didn't bother Maddy. She asked, "So where do we start looking for this new system, Prof.?"

The professor said, "Let's deconstruct the places where the current system is hitting a wall. Identifying the gaps could lead us to probable options. Let's disaggregate, declutter, solve, and then reaggregate. Let's look at these one at a time". And thus, the knight and her guide started exploring the contours of this modern 'Chimera'.

WHAT'S THE PROBLEM ?

"What are the most important or more frequent complaints you receive on your performance system, Maddy?", asked the professor. Maddy had a list of failings she had encountered over the years. She had come prepared.

Employee grouses:
- My L1 manager did not remember all of what I did; s/he had one or more of the biases like recency bias, primacy bias, halo effect, horn effect, anchoring effect, and so on
- My L1 manager's rating was overturned by his/her boss, the L2 manager; this is plain interference
- My L1 manager did not own the rating; s/he said, this was decided by L2 manager or HR or company or someone else.
- HR forced my L1 manager to fit the ratings to a bell curve; my manager made me the scapegoat by reducing my score to fit the bell curve; my colleague escaped with a good rating
- I don't agree with my manager's assessment; the rating and assessment are a surprise
- I am in the wrong category of rating, clubbed with others who are doing far less than me but still are getting the same rating as me
- I am in the right category of rating, but others who are doing far less have been given the same rating as me, they

are in the wrong category
- Ratings are relative, not absolute; there are good years and there are bad years; irrespective of this, I get the same rating every year
- Despite performance ups and downs, forced distribution of the HR stays the same, the percentage distribution remains the same
- Goal setting is delayed; I get nine months to finish my twelve months' goals, but my manager assesses me for the full year

L1 Managers complaints:
- Goal setting is a quarter or so delayed, giving less time to employees to achieve them
- I give frequent advice to the employee throughout the year, but he comes back at the end of the year saying the rating is incorrect / he was never told he would receive a bad rating
- The scale is based on subjective anchors like 'satisfactory' and 'unsatisfactory'; satisfactory for one is unsatisfactory for another; they are meaningless
- The system is relative, not absolute in its measurement; my peer L1 manager is very liberal in rating her team; this forces me to be equally liberal, or else my team will get unfairly low benefits
- The 'Likert Scale' is not helping me the give right feedback to my team; I give 4 out of 5 and yet my employee feels she got less; in fact, anything less than 5 is questioned by the employee, and all 5s are questioned by HR
- My L1 manager overrides my assessment and ratings of my team frequently
- My HR doesn't agree with the ratings I give
- I am forced to punish loyalty; I have to give a low rating to at least a few of my team members by design every year; if my poor performer leaves before the year-end, it is worse; then I have to find another relatively better performer and give a poor rating to maintain the bell curve

HR pain points:
- No one sets their goals on time; it feels like goal setting is an HR goal and no one else's
- L1 managers are positively biased; their rating vis-à-vis performance is very generous
- L1 managers do not like giving poor feedback themselves; while they are always at the forefront, wanting to be the first to give any good news like promotion, good increment, and so on, they push the delivery of unpleasant news like poor rating, PIP, poor increment, missed promotion and so on to HR making HR the bearer of bad news
- L1 & L2 managers tell employees that HR reduced the ratings; they do not take ownership of changes to the ratings; if they had been fair in giving the rating, recalibration would not have been necessary
- The bell curve was supposedly a balanced one, in reality, it's top heavy, with about 20% in the top rating (5 on 5), 40% in the 'significant' category (4 on 5), and the remaining 40% in the 'satisfactory' category (3 on 5). Hardly 1-2% get the '2' rating (needs improvement) and virtually none get the '1' rating.
- Management forces the bell curve even when there are not enough poor performers in a year
- No one takes quarterly check-ins or half-years feedback steps seriously; this is considered a check-box activity
- Managers do not provide development feedback adequately; they do this as a check-box activity
- The performance management system does not differentiate between the good and the poor performers adequately; consequently, the incentive to perform better is little and to perform indifferently is very high
- Everyone believes HR forces employees and managers alike to go through performance management process steps like goal setting, quarterly check-ins, half-yearly feedback, and annual assessment; this makes HR

unpopular among employees

The professors noted everything down. He commented, "There seem to be many gaps in the current system. Let us pick them up one by one and examine the psychology behind these actions. After all, you agree Maddy that the system itself was designed with good outcomes in mind. It's the outcomes that didn't match the design. Let's see what human irrationality we can glean from these that eventually create such dramatic mismatch."

DOES MY SOLDIER KNOW WHAT MY GENERAL WANTS ?

Let me tell you something I had read a while back, said the professor. "The Maratha warrior king Chatrapati Shivaji had a smaller army in comparison to the then dominant force in India, the Moghuls. His army lacked the firepower of the enemy. And yet history tells us that he used the topography of the land in the deccan plateau, the western ghats, and the Vindhya Mountain range right up to the edge of the Gangetic plains to constantly make the enemy defend its territory. Some of the famous battles his army fought and the forts they captured are the stuff of legends. If you go through them, you will find an interesting thread; he wasn't leading his forces in many of these victories. His army command was not in the hands of a single general either, there were many, at least 15 by historical count. And each worked according to his own objective while contributing to the growth and expansion of the Maratha empire.

So, how did Shivaji achieve this?"

Maddy thought and responded, "The Maratha army was famous for its successful use of guerrilla tactics in battle against a larger force. What are you hinting at prof.?"

The prof. said, "I am glad you know that part of history. It is said that every battle is won twice, once in the mind and next on the field. We call it strategy and tactics. Many battles have been lost due to bad strategy; those are pretty famous; books have been written about them. But tell me, will a good strategy alone win you a war?"

"Of course, no. It needs to be implemented as battle tactics."

"And who implements the battle tactics?" asked the professor as if on cue.

"The soldiers of course", replied Maddy.

"And how do the soldiers know the tactics?" asked the professor, continuing to be a step ahead.

Maddy thought and told, "I don't know how, but I can guess that the soldiers are told what to do before the battle, they are given clear instructions."

The professor rounded off her response by adding, "And are given constant updates on the goings on in the battlefield. The army that remains on top of this information knows when and how to adapt to the changes as they happen. In other words, the general's strategy is the solder's tactic and the soldiers' feedback from the battleground is feedback for the generals to upgrade their strategy."

"So, what is the connection here, prof.?", asked Maddy.

"Well, the organization sets the goals at the beginning of the year. It is done at the board level. Then it is cascaded down to every employee for them to draw up their goals and execute. The board i.e. the strategy makers meet every month or at least every quarter to take stock, make course corrections, and reevaluate the assumptions. How much of that update goes down to the last man standing? Are the goals of the soldiers updated to match the revisions in strategy of the generals? Are the employee goals revisited more than once?" The professor stopped at this point.

Maddy had not considered the goals to be an area of concern.

At the beginning of the year, the company goals were set in the shape of a scorecard. The scorecard had major levers like financial objectives, operations parameters, people metrics, and process parameters. All these were the targets of the CEO. In short, the company scorecard was the goal sheet for the CEO. The CEO cascaded the goals down to the CXOs, each of whom then cascaded the same down to their functional or operational teams respectively. The operation heads and the function heads then signed off the scorecards of each team level manager working under them, and such managers then divided the objectives down to the individual contributors. In this manner the CEO down to the frontline staff, all got their goals and objectives set. The performance against the set targets flowed in the reverse with outcome from frontline staff and supervisors upwards adding up to the CEO. The system was robust.

However, the system was not giving the desired results. And the root cause for a good system failing at execution was the lack of the processes to monitor the progress of objectives throughout the year and provide periodic feedback. In the absence of this, the objectives were more like a well-designed textbook that were handed over to the student but in the absence of periodic assessment were leading to some students doing very well at the annual exams while some students doing very poorly / failing at the same exams.

While every school wants to provide the best of textbooks to its students, a school is adjudged the top school when 100% of its students pass and the class aggregate average score is at or above 90%. Even if one of the students in the class fails to clear the tests the school loses its 100% pass rate. And even when the school achieves a 100% pass rate, if many students appear to have passed with second division or worse scores, having entered the club of 100% pass rate, the school still loses out from being among the top. This is a classic example of quantity and quality together bringing success to an institution.

Maddy thought: We have a great way to set our targets. We have a great set of doers and managers. And yet in the absence of periodic review of goals and course correction, we continue to face performance challenges. The periodicity of the review needed to be increased to match the periodicity of the management review and course correction.

She noted this down. She was looking forward to the next battleground the professor was going to choose.

ZEIGARNIK EFFECT

"There is this story of Bluma Zeigarnik, a psychologist", said the professor. "One evening, Zeigarnik and her friends were visiting a restaurant. The dinner there was great. But the highlight was the service of the waiter. He had an amazing memory in recalling everyone's order, as s/he had placed them, including the minor details, without writing anything down. Zeigarnik and her friends were impressed by the waiter's memory.

After dinner, as she was driving back, Zeigarnik discovered that she had left her jacket at the restaurant. She hastily went back, quite sure that the waiter with this amazing memory would help her locate the jacket. To her horror, upon meeting the waiter again, he could not recognize her. She had to remind him that they just had their dinner, and he had waited on them.

While she eventually got her jacket back, the incident got her thinking. Further research on the workings of the human brain led her to the finding that our short-term memory is used to accomplish our short-term tasks. We shift some of those experiences to our long-term memory to be able to recall them in the future. If we have no intention of recalling something in the future, our brain does not process this move. As our short-term memory has limited storage space, our brain hits the delete button when a routine task is completed, and our short-term memory is wiped clean, ready for the next task. What's unfinished remains active, to be finished, and to be deleted immediately afterward to make space for the next task.

And that's how, Zeigarnik found, waiters at restaurants remembered every little detail of the order until the service was complete, and the cheque paid. Then they, or rather their memory, moved on to the next customer and the next cheque.

This phenomenon became known as the Zeigarnik Effect.

This same effect can explain why we forget the key at the door when we open doors, why people forget ATM cards in the card slot after withdrawing money, why people forget originals at the photocopier after photocopying a document, and why managers forget all the hard work done by their team members once the task is accomplished.

Blame it on the Zeigarnik Effect. How tragically fascinating, isn't it?

Now that we know the problem, we can be alert to its effect and find solutions to deal with it. Locks are now coming with the feature of not letting the door open till the key has been pulled out and ATMs are being modified to prompt card removal before cash disbursement. Perhaps it is time, we modified the performance recording system to protect team members and managers alike from the harms of the Zeigarnik Effect in a similar fashion."

Maddy was fascinated.

FILL IT, SHUT IT, RECORD IT !

"Now, if it is in the nature of us humans to store things in our RAM only up till it is useful, we will always have a mismatch in performance vs. assessment", said Maddy. She was beginning to grasp the enormity of the problem. Doing an annual assessment using short-term memory was as easy as doing mental maths. Expecting everyday managers to be 'Shakuntala Devi' was pure incorrect expectation. So, she asked, "Can we not train the managers to record the events regularly? Afterall no one can remember everything from last 12 months, almost no one."

The professor smiled. "You are right, Maddy. The managers must record the performance regularly. And many managers have been smart enough to figure this lacuna. They keep meticulous records of their teams' performance. But think about it; if it is difficult to remember everything for the manager, it is equally difficult to do so for the employee as well. What if the manager records it and narrates the incidents during the annual appraisal to explain the assessment, how much of it will be remembered and concurred by the employee?"

The professor had a point, Maddy thought. The professor always did, that's why he was 'the' professor. Anyways, Maddy came back to the question at hand.

"The employee also needs to record the incidents and the feedback by the manager. While the feedback can be given anytime, it must be recorded on the spot, agreed by the manager and the employee and signed off. It is only then they can have a fair performance conversation at the end of the year."

The prof. prodded, "What if the process of recording is asynchronous? If the incident referred to by the manager and the employee do not match?"

Maddy said, "Then they must go by the one true source, the company records. Afterall, many organizations have started continuous, anytime feedback mechanism. They have created processes / instruments to record these conversations for better and more accurate retrieval. That should solve the problem."

And like a chess grandmaster, the prof. was waiting for Maddy to make that move. He said, "Great, Maddy! So, the organizations seem to have created the right system to overcome the 'Zeigarnik Effect'. Then why are the employees still complaining? At least, that's what the published organization-wide surveys are saying, right?"

Maddy was in a fix. The system was there, feedback was being given at any time during the year. And yet, what the prof. said was also true. If every conversation was generating data points, the aggregate data set should have led to the expected outcome, i.e. individual memory being replaced with organizational memory recorded on an HRIT system. Then why were the outcomes not meeting expectations? She was clueless. But what the prof. said next changed her entire perspective.

The prof. asked, "Is the data generated by organizations statistically valid and reliable?"

And that's when Maddy started to look at the narrative in an entirely different light. The anytime feedback was a great tool. It allowed flexibility, but that meant, the generated data was not collected at comparable periodicity. Some managers were giving feedback once every few weeks, some every few months, some not at all. Statistically this kind of data would fail a split-half reliability test. And those managers that were giving feedback, they were doing so at irregular intervals. This meant that all the feedback given by the same manager to the same employee could not be compared to such feedback by the same manager to another employee in the same team (to check for consistency, another name for reliability). Statisticians call this the test-retest reliability failure. So, while the data generated was huge, it was random and uneven; it was non-parametric. While statisticians love random data - it is the foundation for any data analysis, they need parameterized data, data that is representative of the whole. Stratified random sampling is an example of sample that is random yet representative of the population. Without this characteristic, random data will give a random analysis with a poor correlation with the population. Remember we cannot collect all data (we cannot check every minute of the work done by the employee or every minute of the feedback given by the manager), so we must ensure that the collected data is representative. If it is not, the outcome will throw the analyst off the true value by a large margin. An apt example is the exit poll survey. Psephologists routinely do exit poll surveys before the actual results are out. While the vote-counting in the elections is counting the entire population (every vote), the exit pollsters count only a sample (like one in every 1000 or so) that too not the same votes (those are sealed in ballot boxes) but a rather trust-based response from the sample voter. There have been too many exit poll disasters than one can count, mostly because the sampling is not representative enough of the population. Maddy was a statistician herself.

She was in fact the official statistician between the two. She should have known better.

She understood now that the best part about the anytime feedback was also the 'Achillies Heel' of the system. It did not let the data lend itself to any meaningful analysis.

She looked at the professor with renewed admiration and said, 'Prof. I think we should go for structured periodic feedback. This will ensure each manager provides feedback at the same time interval for each of his/her team members (periodicity) in a pre-defined format (structured). This will help us do comparable analysis across managers within the same period as also for the same manager-employee across different time periods.

The professor just smiled while nodding affirmatively. He said he was reminded of an old advertisement by Hero Honda in the nineties. They had just then launched their motorbikes with high fuel efficiency. To communicate the 80 kmpl mileage of the new model, where 30-40 kmpl mileage was the market norm, they had come up with this tagline, 'Fill it, Shut it, Forget it'. He said it was apt for this situation, 'Fill it, Record it, Forget it' so the record could be retrieved and analyzed anytime in future.

PSYCHOLOGY OF FREE ADVICE

The professor was speaking again. "So, the goals are ever changing, ever evolving. The board knows it. The senior leadership is battling it every month. Goals are becoming obsolete before the yearend, but the employees might still be chasing the old goals set at the beginning of the year. We should update this as often as we need to and communicate to the last man / woman standing.

Then we saw how managers are wired to forget the contributions (or lack of it) of their team members by the time the year is up. To guard against this inevitability, we should record the feedback in a structured manner that is comparable across the organization and at a periodicity that ensures we record the incidents before they lose their relevance (and hence memory) for the managers. Great! So far, so good.

Now the central themes are: how often is often enough? And what structure is structured enough."

Maddy couldn't agree more.

The professor spoke again. "Let's take up one theme at a time. How often should we plan this feedback? You see Maddy, I am just a professor, I teach for a living. You are a professional. You have seen the corporate from close quarters. What is practical in your opinion?"

Maddy knew the prof. was not this humble when on firm ground. This was no faux pas. He was genuinely not sure.

She voiced her opinion. "Organizations already did an annual assessment of performance. It was universal. Some had moved to quarterly assessment as well. Many organizations' commercial businesses did quarterly performance evaluation and even had their performance incentives paid at the end of each quarter. All organizations could move to quarterly assessments as the logical next step. But that would still be a half-hearted effort. First, business changes were coming think and fast. The rate of change of change itself had picked up pace. While quarterly assessments were a definite improvement over the annual assessment, many projects and tasks that employees did these days had a shorter turnaround time. So, the primary aim of managers being able to remember and give accurate feedback would still be unmet at this frequency.

The boards gave monthly feedback to the management in many organisations. If the pace of growth was not that high, it happened at a quarterly frequency. However, the management itself met every month to review the organization performance. There were hardly any organizations left that didn't need their senior management to meet this often. If the organizations were checking in on their progress every month and were doing course correction (as needed) every month, what better way to ensure the immediacy of implementing this change upto the last man / woman in the organization than a monthly assessment!"

While Maddy was on this monologue, she was kind of thinking aloud. When she heard herself say those last few sentences, she couldn't believe it could happen. She just reached the logical conclusion of the line of thought. It sounded logical alright, but not practical. Anyway, she had come to ideate with the professor. Why leave any possibility out?

"Okay", the professor said, "the frequency of feedback, other than annual, can be quarterly or even monthly. But it has to be structured so it could be compared to others feedback within the same time zone and to the same person's feedback across time zones."

Maddy said, "Professor, this frequency thing, I can understand. But what do you mean by the structured feedback? Are you saying the organizations' current practice of giving feedback is not structured? We do not provide any rating during this feedback, sure, but other than that we go the whole hog. I believe this is structured alright." Jousting with the professor was a humbling experience, but this was firm ground for Maddy. She was confident she had done her best as a HR professional. She did not need to feel reticent about it.

The professor was slow to respond. He seemed to be pondering over a subject but not sure how to start. After a long pause he stated, "You are right Maddy. The corporations are fertile ground for experimentation. And you and your colleagues are at the forefront of people practices. I will give you that. While we are at it, let us take a detour and examine a case in point. I assume you have kids."

Maddy nodded in affirmative. An affectionate smile came over her face when she remembered her girl and boy. She was already missing them. The professor continued, "Now they must be growing up fast, passing their learning stages with age. With so many electronic sources of information, the kids of today are more of self-learners than your generation. Many a times this gadget-based self-learning can lead to distractions as well. And there are plenty of them. So, I am guessing you have put some restrictions on their screen time to ensure they do not get addicted and lose focus, right?"

Maddy nodded in affirmative again. Only she knew how hard that was. The professor asked, "So, how do you control their screen time. By telling them to stop after a certain period, right?"

Maddy gave a smug smile. "Sorry, prof. things don't work like that anymore. Your generation probably listened to their parents. Our generation was rebellious, but we did listen to our parents. Else we got a healthy dose of punishment (they both chuckled). But this generation is just unmanageable. Physical punishment is not fashionable anymore. The teachers are not allowed to touch the children let alone punish. We parents get away with a little more than that but just a little more. You can't threaten these kids with such punishment anymore. They are equally impervious to parents telling them that their screentime is up. They just ignore such information. My girl is a little better than my boy. Sometimes she responds with '10 more mins mama' or 'ya, I am switching off' kind of assurances. But when I come back after half an hour, she is still on her screen. They don't seem to care for my cajoling (please stop), logical advice (it is not good for your eyes) or threats (I will cut off the internet). They seem to intuitively know that these are empty threats. They just ignore me and carry on, unmindful."

The professor smiled his cryptic smile. Maddy felt being drawn into a trap, again. But she was releasing her pent-up frustration in dealing with young children. Right then, she couldn't care less.

The professor asked, "So, how do you deal with such situations?"

"Well, after a few trials and errors, I found out that they have some trigger points. My girl loves chocolates, so much so that she ends up eating too much and then having all sorts of problems. So, she is allowed only a fixed quantity a day, not more. I observed that the moment I touch this point, I have her attention. Similarly, my boy loves outdoor games. He is mad about football. That's his trigger point. So, I learnt to ration their screen time with their other favourite factors. Every time I see my girl binging on some series, no more threats, warnings or cajoling; I just say she will be giving up her chocolate quota in lieu of the extra time she spends in front of the screen. Every time my boy is overdoing screentime, I tell him it will come from his outdoor playtime, study time remains unchanged. This gets their attention, total and complete", said Maddy, with a proud smile of a mother having cracked the morse code of her children.

The professor smiled as well. He was ready. "Look Maddy, it is your own experience that children do not listen to any advice, even when it is for their own good, when it is given away free, without any cost attached to it. They do not value it. Give the same advice but with an attached carrot or stick and it works beautifully. While you have given the 'stick' examples, I am sure you would have got positive results with some 'carrot' options as well."

Maddy accepted. The professor continued. "If children with their still-developing minds are already wired to respond to free advice and consequence-based advice differently, should we not expect similar responses from adults, albeit even stronger on both counts."

Maddy thought about it. The professor was right. How

many training programs she had run across different organizations without much success! It was largely due to the lack of consequence if they failed the training. If there was no consequence for failure, there was no seriousness in trying to pass. Training programs had become official time away from work. People came to such programs to de-stress. If this was the case with trainings, why would it be any different with performance feedback. The feedback was a subjective commentary. There was no format, no parameters, just free text response for the manager to fill up and employee to respond to. No wonder it was not being taken seriously.

The professor summed up the reasons for the failure of free advice thus:

a. Value: Anything given free is perceived to have no or low value. The marketing folks know it only too well. That is why one would see premium pricing on goods that have very little additional functional value, but people still buy them at these higher prices and flaunt them as a measure of relative value.

b. Accountability: If advice is given free, it is like 'caveat emptor' or 'buyers beware'. If the advice works, you are in luck. If it doesn't, well, it was free, so don't blame me.

c. Consequence: If free advice has no accountability on the giver, it also has no consequence of non-following for the taker as well.

d. Unsolicited, ego, credibility: if my colleague is getting no feedback from his/her L1 manager and I am getting a lot from my L1 manager, I perceive it as not credible, unnecessary and unwanted.

With this, the professor stopped to check what Maddy thought. It was easy for Maddy to connect with what the prof. said. Just that she kept asking herself, "Why did I not think about it, myself!"

WHAT'S IN A NAME ?

It was time for some tea. The professor had a nice terrace garden, one of the few perks of a campus accommodation. Maddy and the professor were having their tea there. His wife had grown a beautiful patch with a variety of roses.

"A rose by any other name would still smell the same", said Maddy, by way of complementing the gardener. It was a quote from Shakespeare.

"Would it?" Asked the professor, ever alert to seize an opportunity and land a subject, a gift of the gab from years of teaching.

"Yes, of course", said Maddy, never to let an opportunity at winning pass.

"Well, one wouldn't be that confident if one was dealing with humans", said the professor.

"What do you mean, prof.", asked Maddy.

"We need to evaluate frequently and record the achievement of goals as well. Isn't it! While the frequency can be as high as every month, what tools do we use to evaluate?"

"We have our trusted 'Likert Scale' to help us record the achievements, right? Why not trust it with the job on a monthly basis as well?" asked Maddy.

And off they moved to an in-depth discussion on the 'Likert Scale'.

LIKERT CALLING WHERE ARE YOU?

"What kind of rating scale is good, 1-2-3-4-5, 5-4-3-2-1, 1-2-3, 3-2-1, 1-2-4-5 (a variation of 5-point scale without the median) or some other combination? What would be the best scale for use? Or are there horses for courses?", asked Maddy.

The professor said, "The industry predominantly favours the five-point scale i.e. the 1-2-3-4-5 scale. For some, 1 denotes the best performance and for others it's the worst. This way companies distribute individual performances across these five levels.

However, something everyone agrees with is that *the rating scale has no numeric meaning.*

If we look at 1 as the best performance, it relates to the meaning of being the 'numero uno'. On the other hand, mathematically, it would have meant 1 out of 5, i.e. only 20%. Similarly choosing 5 as the best performance level would mean the highest (among available) level. It denotes the highest level of performance like in a game where we start with level 1 and move to level 2 and so on till, we reach the final level. In this case fifth level is the final level. However, 5 is not the universally accepted top level. The decimal system uses 10 as the top level, the percentage system uses 100 as the top level, the Olympics system uses 1 as the top performer and so on for each cohort of users.

So, in both systems of rating, the rating scale has relative positional value but no numeric meaning. This has been a problem for the financial decisions. When the rating scales are used for various purposes that involve financial decision-making, HR folks usually convert the scale into a set of numeric decision levers. For example, the rating one is converted into five so that the employees rated one can receive five times a basic level of benefit compared to the lowest rating. If the reverse scale is used, the five rated employees receive the highest proportional benefit like merit increase and so on.

With all the benefits of clubbing performances into homogeneous groups and differentiating rewards and recognition across groups, comes the downside of not being able to differentiate the employees within a group.

Employee performance does not involve simple five levels, it is like a spectrum of colours, an array of outcomes. It involves employee-to-employee difference in performance and within an employee month-on-month variation in performance. A 5-point scale does not do enough justice. So, some companies expand the scale to include two more levels making it a 7-point measurement scale. These are the challenges of managing annual performance. Let us say we look at a short period of one month's performance for each employee and aggregate 12 such monthly performances. Then we are faced with two unique situations. The first one is that unlike the yearly cycle, the performance of people during short periods of one month does not come out to be very wide in the range. There can be three possibilities: the person may do the job as expected or the person may do the job less than the expectation or the person may in fact do a job that is more than the expectation. This way there can be a 3-point rating scale for such scenario. The second one is: as we add more and more months, we need to add three new possible outcomes for every month added. So, for a 12-month period we will have a range of scores starting with the lowest possible rating for all of the 12 months and ending with the highest possible rating for all of the 12 months. In terms of numbers, if we use a scale of 1-2-3 with one being the lowest and three being the highest score in a month, we will end up with a minimum score of 12 and a maximum score of 36 for the year. As you would have observed by now, the scale has moved from being a 5-point rating scale to a whooping 25-point rating scale starting with 12 and ending with 36.

This is a big problem to handle. What do we do now?"

Maddy was lost for words. The professor, however, was on to something.

"If you look at the number of possibilities it may look like there are 25 variations. However, unlike the annual process where we need to give the ratings only once, at the end of the year, in this process we need to give the ratings every month. This makes getting a high or a low rating that much more difficult in a short period of time.

Let me put it another way. Let us say we have a person receiving the highest rating at the end of a year, a '5' rating. What is not obvious is that this automatically means that the person received a '5' rating for the entire year or 12 months in the year. While this is not obvious at first glance, when we look at it from this angle, we realize it is impossible for an employee to be at the peak performance level all year round, every day, every month. However, because we created the system that gives feedback only once in an entire year, there is no other option but to differentiate people in this manner. If we take the exact opposite possibility, it will look even more outlandish. The person receiving the lowest rating, let us say rating '1' out '5' at the end of one year, will mean that the person was perennially at the very bad performance level throughout the 12 months of the year. If we look at the rating from this perspective, first of all, we will realize that this is not true. Just like the best performance for the year does not mean it was best throughout the year, poor performance for the entire year does not mean the performance is at the same level every month of the year.

The process of arriving at an annual final rating is an exercise in finding the average performance for the year.

This means the high performer for the year at '5' rating must be higher or lower than '5' during the months leaving us with a mean performance of '5'. Therefore, the person might in fact have fluctuated from any level of performance like '1' or '2' or '3' or '4' or even beyond '5'. This way the average comes to '5'. Similarly, the poor performance must have had periods of higher and lower performance than '1', bringing the average to '1'. So, what looks like a five-points rating scale is in fact a much wider scale being averaged out to the final scale of 5 levels.

Let us draw tabular and graphic representations of how each of the annual average ratings move during the course of the year."

Annual Rating	Rating 1	Rating 2	Rating 3	Rating 4	Rating 5
Month 1	1	2	3	4	5
Month 2	2	1	2	3	4
Month 3	-1	3	2	6	4
Month 4	-3	2	3	7	3
Month 5	1	1	2	2	1
Month 6	3	0	3	4	5
Month 7	1	-1	4	4	6
Month 8	1	2	4	4	5
Month 9	4	3	1	2	6
Month 10	2	3	3	5	7
Month 11	1	5	5	4	8
Month 12	0	3	4	3	6
Avg. (Annual) Rating	**1**	**2**	**3**	**4**	**5**

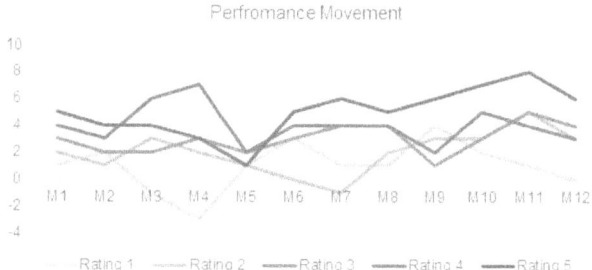

Maddy had never looked at it from this perspective. However, having come to know now, she couldn't deny the validity of the professor's analysis. No wonder everyone cribbed that they are being incorrectly slotted in the rating scale. The scale was inadequate to start with.

BELL THE LIKERT

It was becoming increasingly clear that the best scale for a 12-month monthly system would be a 3-point rating scale with 'achievement of outcome' being the midpoint and 'not achieving' and 'overachieving' on the two sides. Then came the challenge of defining a scoring system. While the descriptions had reached a fair level of maturity, the challenge of providing a numeric tag to each of these performance anchors, remained unaddressed.

The choice of going by the popular 'Likert' rating scale was obvious. That would mean giving numeric tags of 1, 2, 3 to below expected outcome, expected outcome and above expected outcome respectively. However, there was this flaw: 1, 2 and 3, by themselves lent themselves to very little meaning besides informing the reader that a score of '1' was less than score of '2' and so was '2' than '3'. This was comparative scoring at its best and confusing numeric tags at its worst.

Another option would be inverting the scoring to tag '3' to 'below expected outcome' and tagging '1' to 'above expected outcome'. This would be the classic case of 'podium finish' performance tags and easy to understand for the users. The catch in this system, however, was that the podium finish scores were an end in themselves. They did not lend themselves to the computation of outcomes at an aggregate level. That was not the case in performance outcomes.

An example would illustrate this better. Suppose the system with '1' being the best performance and '3' being the worst was adopted. At the end of the year, a person with consistent best performance would have got a score of 12 out of 12 months and the worst performer on a consistent basis would have scored 36 out of 12 months. While a podium finish score of 1 in a year would make it look like the achiever, a score of 12 in a year would be lost in translation.

So, what would be an alternative scoring system that would maintain the three point Likert scale, be representative of the performance descriptors and be amenable to mathematical calculations needed to convert performance scores into useful decision leavers like merit increases or performance-based bonuses or career progression decisions and such other process outcomes?

While pondering over this issue, Maddy thought to herself: When it is said that a person has achieved the outcome at expected level, in financial terms it is mentioned as 100% achievement. This was quite familiar to the people working in commercial segment of organisations. They were routinely reviewed on their performance reaching 100% and were paid performance bonuses upon doing so. For those with stretch goals, an achievement of 90% (say) would in fact be achievement of the goals, leading to initiation of payout of performance bonus. The higher the stretch target the lower would be the percentage at which the organisation would deem to have achieved its goals and start the performance bonus payout.

Accordingly, 90%-100% range could be the baseline around which the lower and higher performances could be calibrated. Less than 90% performance would be rated as 'not achieved' the goals and anything exceeding 100% would be deemed as a 'performance exceeding expectation'. The range of 90%-100% could be the range for 'at-par' performance.

While this was common in the commercial side of organisation due to their quarterly or monthly performance reviews, it was equally uncommon among the operations and R&D part of the organisations due to their annual frequency of appraisal. It was time to bring the best of both worlds together. The three-point rating scale that was already in plans could pick up the numeric scores of the best rating system available to the world when it came to frequent performance review system; one that converts the performance scores to performance outcomes like rewards and recognitions seamlessly.

Maddy outlined them:
1. The organisation can decide the level of difficulty incorporated into its score card. Based on this, the minimum completion status in terms of percentages can be set as the cut off at or above which an employee is deemed to have achieved the goals; let us say this is 90%. Then 90% becomes the base level performance for receiving a 'goals achieved' status or the mid-point on a three-point scale. Upon achievement of 90%-100% performance, 100% performance score is given. In Microsoft excel, a cell with 100% percentage value when converted to numeric value gave out 1 and vice versa, so this was logical. In other words, the performance score for 90%-100% achievement is 1.
2. Those failing to achieve 90% i.e. 89% or below receive 'goals not achieved' status or 0.
3. Those achieving more than 100% i.e. 101% and above receive 'goals achieved and exceeded' status or 2.

This time, it was the professor who was impressed with Maddy.

THE PSYCHOLOGY OF ZERO

Maddy and the professor were able to zero in on a 3-point scale while simultaneously getting the scale to communicate the performance levels accurately and seamlessly. What's more, the scores were now amenable to mathematical calculations as well. This was a necessity to convert performance into subsequent actions related to rewards and recognitions. A few examples would be apt here.

An employee doing a 'poor job' or 'not achieving' the desired results would receive a zero score for that month. This would tell the employee immediately that his or her job was not up to the mark.

An employee achieving results as per the expectations would receive a score of one. This would send out the message that the employee was at or close to 100% of his/her job. In situations where an employee might have exceeded 90% of job expectation but not met 100% of it, a one score could still be awarded. The 10% tolerance would provide for all minor variations in job performance that still help the organisation achieve its long-term objectives and penalize a performer for narrow misses. In case an organisation sets its targets that are quite achievable, it could set itself a range of, let us say, 95% to 105% performance to award the score of one i.e. 'at par' performance.

And the last of the three scenarios: if an employee achieved more than 100%, s/he would be judged to have achieved and exceeded the outcomes. This would mean a disproportional reward of a score of two for that month.

If organizations set achievable targets (as opposed to a stretch target), they could modify the ranges to reflect this philosophy. They could set 94% or below as 'not achieved' or '0', 95%-105% as '1' or 100% at par performance and '106% or more' as '2' or above par performance.

"In this manner", Maddy said, "we can implement a monthly performance review system based on a 3-point rating scale". The professor nodded in agreement.

LOST & (NOT) FOUND

"Great work up till now, Maddy", said the professor. It was noon; they took a break. Lunch was a quiet affair; each being lost in thoughts from the morning. After lunch, they went out for a walk around the campus.

The professor said, "We have looked at goals, frequency of check-ins, structure of check-in, and the rating-scoring system as well. We looked at the psychology of the manager in assessing the team members' performance. Now, let us examine the system from the eyes of the team member, the employee, shall we?" Maddy nodded in acceptance. The professor continued, "Do you know the story of Abraham Wald and 'Survivor Bias'?" Maddy answered in negative. The professor narrated it in brief.

"This is a famous story from WWII. The Germans and the British were fighting a fierce war of attrition in the skies. Planes from both sides would conduct frequent raids and bomb each other's cities and facilities in order to gain an upper hand. The price paid was equally high with several aircrafts getting hit with bullets and falling off the sky along with loss of life of the pilots.

The Brits wanted to thicken the armour plating of the aircraft body to reduce the man-machine losses. But the extra weight would cause reduced mileage endangering their return or worse, forced landing in enemy territory. The decision was made: Analyse the returning planes for bullet hole patterns and double plate the most critical parts of the plane. This would ensure increased safety and fuel efficiency, both.

The engineers got down to business. They analysed the bullet holes from the returning planes and for sure a pattern emerged.

It was obvious the fuselage and the wings were taking the maximum hits. These had to be protected with double plating. But just before the results were to be presented, Abraham Wald, one of the researchers on that team asked something like: 'Is this all the input? Have we analysed all the planes that went out on the raids?'

The answer was a clear 'no'. The Navy was losing far too many planes to bullets. That was the original reason for the research. So, analysis of the ones that returned meant that the fuselage and wings were taking the maximum hits and still returning. They would continue to return even without further protection.

The parts that, upon taking a bullet, did not survive to return and tell their story were the places that needed that extra plating. In other words, the parts in the pattern that had no bullet holes were the places that needed protection. A bullet there was fatal to the plane and the pilot, both. No wonder they were the cockpit and the fuel tank. So, the story goes, the plating was done as per recommendation, and sure enough more planes started returning from their sorties.

"What's this story got to do with the employee performance?" Asked Maddy. "A lot", said the professor.

"Performance management is a process that runs in lockstep with the business cycle. The business cycle runs on an annual basis, in some organisations, based on the calendar year, and in most, based on the financial year. The process follows the standard three-step cycle of input-processing-output.

The Input (Goal Setting): the business goals are set at the beginning of a performance cycle say in April of an FY. This creates a cascade of 'goal setting' from business to people, from the top of the hierarchy down to the bottom of the pyramid, from the leaders to the frontline staff. The goals, thus set, become the input data for that performance cycle. The goals become the basis for the performance measurement yardstick at the end of the year. Nothing unusual here.

The Processing: As the months and the quarters pass, organisations keep track of the progress of this performance, i.e. business performance, and provide feedback to both the investors and the management to help them know if the organisation is on track to achieve its goals or is slipping. If the management observes any slippage, it tries to buckle up to make up for lost ground. This is a classic management information system or MIS job.

Nothing unusual here as well, except that organisations are living, breathing entities with people coming in and going out all the time. Those who start the ball rolling at the beginning of the cycle may move on, may be asked to move on, or may even be moved out and their place taken by others with similar skill sets. Organisations call it transfers or attrition with different sub-classes: voluntary, involuntary, regrettable, non-regrettable, desirable, undesirable, etc.

The Output (Annual Performance Appraisal): By the time the cycle ends, a year would have passed as also a lot of water under the bridge. The organisations sign off the business performance, plan vs. actual, to determine how they performed that year. This forms the basis of the annual financial reporting, stock price movements, performance appraisal of employees, merit-based salary increases, performance rewards, and performance improvement plans as consequences."

"So where is the catch? What are the missing planes here?" asked Maddy, attentive as always.

"Well, all organisations try to ensure that they do an equitable and fair job. All the upsides that did not come from business efforts are classified as one-time gains and credit is not passed on to employees. All the misses that were missed due to externalities even when full efforts were put in by the employees, are discounted appropriately while doing individual performance evaluations. All those who joined during the course of the year are treated for the period of their contribution only and all those who worked for the full year are treated with full-year weightage. All this is equitable and fair.

But what about those who were part of the team but moved before the evaluation period ended? They may have contributed during their time or not as the case may be. There can be regrettable exits of performers, non-regrettable exits of non-performers, involuntary exits on account of performance, or any other. All in all, they are the planes that took off but did not return when the day ended, proverbially speaking; our missing planes."

"So what?" Asked Maddy. This was routine. She had

done this every year. No surprises there. But what the professor said next was very interesting.

"The organisations cannot reward the leavers anyways. The performance evaluation happens at the end of the cycle; meaning, there is no record of performance evaluation if a person leaves after goal setting but before cycle closure, the evaluation being a one-time, once-in-a-year, end-of-the-year exercise. On the same note, an organisation cannot disincentivize the poor performers that have left in the middle of a performance cycle by giving them a penalty at the end simply due to the facts that:
a) The person is not there to receive it
b) The poor performance is never recorded till the cycle is over, so there's no 'poor performer' exit before the year.

While the arguments sound logical and ridiculous at the same time, they have stood the test of time and legal challenges.

That brings us to the next question: Unlike the missing planes, our missing employees are not creating any errors of judgement, or are they? Think about it: the organisation loses all kinds of performers, good, average and poor. If the proportion of the loss is equal to the population proportion, i.e. the exits are also a normal distribution just like those that remain, there's no change in the performance distribution at the beginning, during, and at the end of the year.

Remember our discussion about normal distribution and parametric tests, Maddy? The problem starts when that's not the case. In many years and for many organisations, those who leave on account of poor performance are far less in proportion to those who do even when they do well. The proportion is, in fact, below the forced distribution proportion that organisations set for themselves.

In simple words, non-performers do not leave, performers do. This is one of the primary reasons organisations come up with forced distribution to identify and let go of poor performance at a certain rate every year. Sounds logical, right?

But there's the catch. Living, breathing entities metamorph continuously. Evaluating them using static rules is fraught with risk. Let's examine two scenarios:
a) What happens in those years when there are more than proportional non-performing exits? It turns the process on its head; all those that were not good have left, but the system says: weed out a certain percentage at the end of the year, so off go that percentage of employees, more and more of them being incorrectly identified as poor performers.
b) What happens when the system set in place works a few cycles and successfully removes the non-performers? Now the general performance level of those remaining is higher than the market, assuming others haven't followed suit. But what's set in motion can't be pulled back. So off go another set of people next year, this time possibly good performers as per market standards but unlucky to be at the bottom of organisation performance levels. In such cases, both the organisation and the employees are losers. There are no winners here.

We need a system that is agile enough to move in lockstep with the organisation's evolving performance expectation and dynamic enough, at the same time, to respond to changing performance demographics of the employee population."

Maddy understood. It made sense but it was not practical. What system could be agile, dynamic, and yet scientific and reliable? After all this was people being discussed.

HOTEL CALIFORNIA !

The professor and Maddy were in a dilemma. They knew that employees came and went throughout the year. There was no way their performance could be judged at the end of the year if they had already left. First, they were not in the system to receive the feedback. Second, managers would inevitably give them poor ratings as this would help them meet the bell curve distribution without taking a hit for their existing employee base. The managers had become adept at gaming the system, and no one seemed to mind. The same employee whom the L1 manager would move heaven and earth to retain would be judged as a 'poor performer' by the same L1 manager post-separation. This was a classic case of 'grapes having turned sour'.

That's when it struck Maddy like a thunderbolt. Why not use the monthly performance assessment they had been discussing for some time. The system could record the monthly performance. It had numeric performance anchors instead of graphic or positional anchors. That made it easy for employees to understand their performance assessment with minimal reference material: '1' would mean target achieved or 100%, '2' would mean target achieved and exceeded, '0' would mean performance falling short of the target even after accounting for some shortfall buffer. This would ease the life of managers. And most importantly, the monthly scores given to employees would stay around up till the end of the year (and beyond) irrespective of the choices employees made during the year. Some possibilities came to her mind at once:

1. No positive cross-subsidization: Let us say the manager gave a very good rating ('2') to an employee in a month. Next month, the employee decided to resign due to reasons other than work. The manager could not go back and say that this employee was not good. Consequently, the good rating was not reallocated simply to motivate the remaining employees. The other employees had no disadvantage as well. They would continue to receive their share of benefits. It was just that the undue share of benefits could no longer be passed on to any employee basis the likes or dislikes of the manager.

2. No negative cross-subsidization: Let us say the manager gave a very poor rating ('0') to an employee in a month. If, unfortunately, the employee did not recover the lost ground, s/he was likely to receive another '0' on account of next month's performance as well. This served as an automatic performance improvement plan (PIP) for employees. If there were three consecutive 0s, the employee might leave on his/her own volition or might be required to move on as per organization policies. While this was unfortunate, recording this during the months and letting go of the poor performer during the year didn't affect others during the end-of-year performance assessment: no need to find a 'scapegoat' underperformer to match the bell curve (that reminded Maddy, they had to deal with the bell curve as well, but that's for later).

So, the remaining employees in this system would continue to receive their share of benefits as per their performance. The undue share of 'poor performance' was no more needed to be passed on to other employees basis the likes or dislikes of the manager or forced distribution demands of the HR.

Maddy had a detailed discussion with the prof. on these lines. He was impressed by Maddy's idea. He said, "You know Maddy, listening to this idea of yours reminds me of the song 'Hotel California' by the Eagles. The last line goes something like, 'You can check out any time you like, but you can never leave'."

Maddy was left speechless at how the professor, as if on cue, came up with this one-liner aptly describing the system.

ATTENTION ! (BELL) CURVE AHEAD !!

The professor and Maddy came back after their long walk. With so much speaking throughout the day, both were tired. The professor retired to his quarters for a short nap. Maddy promised she would be back for evening tea before walking back to the campus guesthouse. She kept ruminating over what was spoken and what remained.

Evening tea was a quiet affair. Maddy spoke at last, "Professor, I cannot thank you enough for the insights and guidance. Together, we eviscerated our current performance management system in search of a better working model. I discovered some impressive aspects that I am going to go back and implement. However, I believe the centre piece of the jigsaw, the 'bell curve', has not moved even by an inch. I cannot see how we can address this reviled aspect of the annual performance system anytime soon.

Making the goals agile and responsive to changes will be a great move. Allowing managers to record their feedback month on month will address the recency bias. Ensuring that the feedback given by managers is backed by ratings every month will make the employees sit up and take notice of the feedback, this is an excellent idea. Switching from 'Likert scale' to 'Numeric Scale', will usher in the concept of 100% and swing the performance around 100%. This will sharpen the focus of the team on achieving 100%, a great anchor. The one idea I liked most was that of recording scores for everyone whether present at the end of an annual cycle or leaving mid-way. This will ensure we don't lose any performance data points and do not try and find scapegoats at the yearend. All this is great.

However, when we aggregate the performance for the full year, say, by adding up the monthly performances, we will find the distribution to be uneven. That is when the forced distribution will have to be enforced. Let me take up an illustration if you don't mind."

The professor nodded. Maddy continued. "Let us say we adopt the scoring system of '2', '1', '0'. Let us say we have 100 people to be evaluated (representing 100%). If we run the monthly assessment, each month there will be some 0s, some 1s, and the rest 2s. Expectedly, there will be more 2s than 0s. Let me draw up a sample case.

Month	'0' Score	'1' Score	'2' Score
Apr	10	70	20
May	15	60	25
Jun	12	70	18
Jul	3	80	17
Aug	7	70	23
Sep	7	82	11
Oct	10	68	22
Nov	7	78	15
Dec	10	77	13
Jan	8	77	15
Feb	2	80	18
Mar	4	76	20
Annual Avg	7.9	74.0	18.1

As we can see the scores are not evenly distributed. There are few (about 8%) who haven't performed as per expectation and about 18% who have done exceedingly well. This is the scenario during most years with most organizations. Managers, by design, are an optimistic lot. So, HR comes in and does the most hated job, normalization. In the process, some of the 18% high performers get recalibrated to the median scale (1) and some 1s get pushed down to 0 thereby bringing some sanity back. While there is no way to tell if the right pullbacks have been undertaken, the managers and HR try, and do the best job they can, however distasteful it might be.

And before I stop, let me pre-empt the question: What if we don't do normalization? Let us say, we don't normalize; some have already discarded the entire 'bell curve' thing, what's the worst that could happen? Well, as organizations that have removed the concept are finding out, more and more employees are categorised as high performers. In our illustration previously, the 18% can continue going further up and 8% further down if left unchecked. Ultimately this has led the organization to discard ratings themselves as impractical, a classic case of 'throwing the baby with the bathwater'. Hence, I rest my case, we have no alternative to 'bell curve' for now."

With this, Maddy stopped to catch her breath. The professor was listening keenly of course. He handed over a glass of warm water to her and let her settle down for what he was going to say next.

SWING THE BELL

Prof. Sai Nathan started with a measured pace.

"The famous 'Bell Curve' is most possibly as old as the performance management system itself. Do you know how we arrived at this 'Bell' curve? Legend has it that the first 'Bell curve' was not an invention; it was rather a discovery of a common phenomenon found all around us. Let us take a few examples.

If we plot the height of all the people we meet during a day, we will possibly end up with a large number of people with heights close to each other, and a few that are less than this close set, and another few that are more than this close set. If we plot them on a graph, we will end up with a bell-shaped curve.

If we take the IQ of a large number of people, guess what we will end up with, a 'Bell' curve.

If we take examples from nature, we find the tree canopy distribution in the forest to be in the form of a bell. If we plot the species in a natural habitat against their absolute numbers, it will throw up a bell curve once again.

In fact, it is so common a distribution pattern found in both natural and human data sets that scientists call it "normal distribution" as well. It is completely 'normal' to find a bell-shaped distribution pattern.

As long as the data collected is sufficiently large (statisticians believe it to be 30 or more), is random (no match fixing please) and is representative of the population, plotting the data and getting a bell-shaped curve will be a confirmation of sorts that you have done a fair job in data collection.

So how did such a simple, natural, common phenomenon come to represent such a vile angle in people's performance? Let's explore.

Let's plot the distribution of male height in the US during the 1900s. Now if we repeat this at every 10-year intervals leading up to the 1980s, we will get a table and a graph like this (he drew them). We will continue observing the heights to have a normal distribution. Hence, the phenomenon of normal distribution of large-scale data points with sufficient randomness is proven once again.

Height (cm)	1900s	1910s	1920s	1930s	1940s	1950s	1960s	1970s	1980s
164	1%								
165	5%								
166	7%	1%							
167	11%	5%	1%	1%					
168	13%	7%	5%	5%					
169	15%	11%	7%	7%					
170	16%	13%	11%	11%	1%				
171	15%	15%	13%	13%	5%	1%	1%		
172	13%	16%	15%	14%	7%	5%	5%	1%	
173	11%	15%	16%	16%	11%	7%	7%	5%	1%
174	7%	13%	15%	16%	13%	11%	11%	7%	5%
175	5%	11%	13%	13%	15%	13%	13%	11%	7%
176	1%	7%	11%	11%	16%	15%	15%	13%	11%
177		5%	7%	7%	15%	16%	16%	15%	13%
178		1%	5%	5%	13%	15%	16%	16%	15%
179			1%	1%	11%	13%	13%	15%	16%
180					7%	11%	11%	13%	15%
181					5%	7%	7%	11%	13%
182					1%	5%	5%	7%	11%
183						1%	1%	5%	7%
184								1%	5%
185									1%

CATCHING CHIMERA

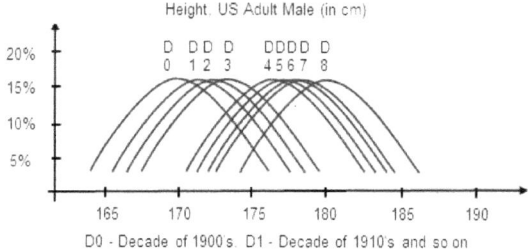

While the distribution is indeed in the shape of a bell curve, the curve itself is not static, it is moving continuously to the right as we move across the timelines. Did you observe that? In simple words, while the height of US citizens is distributed normally, the distribution itself is moving towards more height with time, i.e. 'the average height of US citizens is increasing with every passing decade'.

Timeline	1900s	1910s	1920s	1930s	1940s	1950s	1960s	1970s	1980s
Avg. Height (cm)	170.0	172.1	173.1	173.4	176.1	177.1	177.3	178.3	179.0

Speaking of height, it is interesting to note that this phenomenon is observed in direct correlation with many different factors such as average income, the average amount of protein in the diet, the average life expectancy, etc. across not just the US but universally, from the Roman times to the modern days, from the Americas to Asia and from Siberian tribes to the African tribes."

"So, what's the relation between the above illustrations and 'people performance' in businesses?" asked Maddy.

"Well, guess what?", the professor said, "Businesses are known to give different results during different years. Some businesses have a cyclical nature with outcomes going positive and negative repetitively. Some businesses see very rapid growth followed by tepid growth. Some others have consistently increasing growth in output, a rarity. Still, some other businesses have erratic ups and downs in output basis multiple factors.

However, when we observe the performance of people in different industries and different companies and during different years, what do we see? A beautiful bell curve with poor performers, expected performers, and high performers all sitting neatly across the curve indicating an average of 100% outcome.

In other words, irrespective of the wide variance in business performance going from, say 50% to 150% during different years and in different companies, the people across different companies, sectors, and years are supposedly performing at the same static 100%. What can be more divergent from reality!

No wonder, it has failed the HR folks, the people managers, the organisations, and most importantly the people who have been unfairly evaluated. As the saying goes, 'The road to hell is paved with good intentions'."

"So, what's the solution?" Asked Maddy, hooked by now.

The professor said, "Well! The solution is right in front of us, rather right preceding this revelation of the unnatural static inertia of the 'HR Bell Curve'; if the average height of people can be plotted as a bell curve within a timeline but is seen to move in its entirety when seen over multiple timelines, *why can't the people performance curve move with business performance!*

If we ensure that the mean percentage value of the performance curve matches with the mean percentage value of the business curve it will unfreeze the 'Bell Curve' and let it move fluidly in sync with the business performance. A few illustrations are in order.

Scenario one: Let's say the business performance has been recorded at 100% for the time period. Now the performance graph while continuing to be a bell moves to 100% mean value. This will mean proportional performance categories of 'below par', 'at par', and 'above par' performance groups.

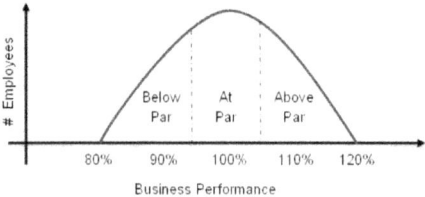

Scenario two: If the business performance for the time period is 90%. We must allow the performance curve to move leftward to ensure the mean coincides with 90% value. This will mean, more people receiving 'below par' rating and proportionally less people receiving 'at par' or 'above par' rating.

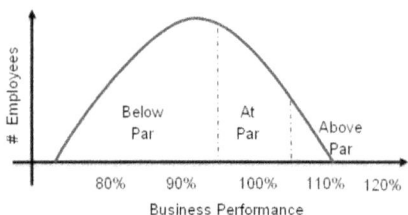

Scenario three: Let's say, the business performance has been recorded at 110% for the time period. Now the performance graph while continuing to be a bell moves over 100% to stop at 110% mean value. This will mean many more performers landing in 'above par' category i.e. 'met and exceeded expectation' category. Simultaneously the proportion of people 'below par' will fall to compensate for the bulge at the top; and rightfully so.

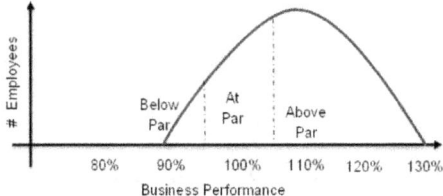

Aren't these scenarios obvious, logical, and natural? If yes, then the solutions will stand the test of scrutiny by business as well."

"Voila!", said Maddy. "The Bell curve is back to being what it is; a normal phenomenon that is now used in lockstep with business results as would any natural, normal distribution would." Maddy and the professor were happy with this discovery. But one thought kept gnawing at Maddy. She intended to ask the professor about it before the day ended.

BOSS PROPOSES SUPERBOSS DISPOSES

The professor was speaking again. "Now that we are looking at strengthening the system of recording the assessment, it should follow the standard process of 'maker-checker-reviewer' principle of error proofing. In human transactions, it helps protect the outcome against individual biases at each stage as well. So, the assessment of the L1 manager in the form of rating or feedback should be double-checked and signed off by the L2 manager, right?"

Maddy nodded in affirmative. The professor continued. "Then, let me narrate an incident from a client HR I had consulted. I was working with one of the large retailers in the country. The HR there had called me requesting my advice in getting out of a tricky situation.

The story went thus: There was this employee who had finished the full performance cycle. She was given a rating by her L1 manager, and it went for review by the L2 manager. They followed the annual performance cycle. The L2 manager had very good visibility of the team's performance or at least he thought he did. During the discussion with the HRBP, the L2 manager believed that the rating given by the L1 manager for this employee was not an accurate reflection of the employee's performance. He changed the rating. The HRBP updated the records. When the L1 manager received the ratings for communication and sign-off by employees, he noticed the change. He called up the HRBP and asked if it was a typographical error. When HR informed him that it was changed by his boss, things came to a head. It seems the L1 manager had already had some grouse against the L2 manager. He quickly raised a complaint to the Head of HR and alleged the HRBP's complicity as well. Later it was found out that the L1 manager was already in possession of an opportunity and was waiting for his performance bonus to resign and move out. That aside, when an official complaint was lodged, the L2 manager had no choice but to accept that he changed the rating without consultation with L1 manager of the employee in question. He alleged the HRBP didn't inform him about any violation in the process. That is where my guidance was sought by the client HR.

While this was a bit of an extreme outcome given the context of the L1 manager willing to kick the matter up, in most such cases the L1 managers simply hand over the rating to the employee. Upon being asked for justification either by the employee (if the rating is less than expected) or by other fellow employees (who might feel a sense of unfair treatment), the L1 manager would simply redirect them to the L2 manager saying, 'Why don't you go ask him? He is the one taking all the decisions'."

The professor ended the narration with a question. "While my advice to my client was situational, the incident brings us back to the contentious question: Who's the Boss?"

Maddy had no response. Her experience was no different.

BOSS IS RIGHT !
WHEN IN DOUBT, GO BACK TO BOSS

The professor continued, "The organisation gives the L1 manager, the responsibility of managing his/her team, if the L1 manager shoulders this responsibility all through the year and the L1 manager's own performance is judged based on the performance of his/her team's performance, why does the system allow the L2 manager to take matters into his/her own hand and intervene directly!

As the manager of the L1 manager, the L2 manager has the duty and responsibility to monitor the supervisory capabilities of the L1 manager. That's the reason in the three-stage process of 'maker', 'checker', and 'reviewer', the L2 manager has the job of reviewing the L1 manager's job, not taking over, and doing the L1 manager's job.

So, the L2 manager should rightfully review the performance assessment done by the L1 manager, not the performance of the employee itself. If s/he disagrees, s/he should discuss this with the L1 manager. If the L1 manager is convinced that the rating should change, s/he would go back and revisit the rating, but this time take ownership of the change. This would be a powerful difference from the past: the change in rating would, instead of being viewed as interference, be appreciated as skill enhancement for the L1 manager in assessing performance. When the employee finally received the rating, the L1 manager would be well placed to explain and help the employee own the rating up as well.

On the other hand, if the L1 manager is able to convince the L2 manager that s/he has done the right evaluation, an error of judgement from someone who's two steps away from the execution would be avoided. It would do yeoman service to the employee, the L1 manager, the L2 manager, and the organisation by keeping the performance evaluation accurate and avoiding all the friction that is acknowledged as the cause of heavy loss of productivity, attrition, a blemish on the performance culture of the organisation, and ultimately, loss of business.

Here are the two golden responses to the question of 'who is the boss?'
The L1 manager is the boss.
And when in doubt, consult the L1 manager, because the L1 manager 'is' the boss."

Maddy smiled at the way the professor had stated a simple solution to one of the most persistent problems of performance assessment. What she couldn't stop thinking to herself was: Why hadn't she thought about this, herself!

"Let us break for dinner", said the professor. Maddy was hungry from all the ideations. She was glad for the offer. She hadn't forgotten the question she wanted to ask the prof, though.

SHAWSHANK (NO) REDEMPTION

The nights were pretty quiet on the campus. The campus was huge, so the buildings were made with a lot of space in between. The student hostels were the islands of noise, music blaring out of someone's speakers, surround sound surrounding the entire block, someone or the other shouting out to someone else, mini gangs of boys and girls roaming around immersed in their own worlds, couples chatting quietly here and there, canteen lights staying on late into the night, action moving to the café next door from midnight to early mornings and so on. But the vast spaces in between meant you could hear the chirping of crickets, occasional hooting of owls, and a lot of silence if you cared to.

The professor was back at the terrace garden with Maddy in tow. At dinner, the professor's wife had commented something about her being a pest. Why couldn't they leave him alone at least during the holidays? Maddy knew she was right. Maddy was eating into their family time. Maddy knew her from her college days. Competing for the professor's timeshare had made her pretty blunt with the students but she had a heart of gold and the kitchen of goddess Lakshmi. Every one of the professor's students knew this. So, they would purposefully try to meet him at the quarters so they could lay their hands on some home-cooked delicacies, except that it came at the price of listening to her complaints about stealing her husband's time. The professor had adjusted to it as the students.

In the silence of the night, Maddy broached the last topic for the day. She said, "Professor, you must recall how we started the morning. You asked me to list down all the problems I faced on account of the performance management system, and I did. We have tackled each of the aspects with some solutions in sight. I will go back and try them. The proof of the pudding will be in eating it. If they worked at the R&D centre, at the operations sites, in commercial teams, and at the corporate centre, we would know we have found workable solutions. Else we have to come back to the drawing board. I am willing to invest that energy.

However, there is one thing that I have not been able to sort in my mind. I wish to untie this last knot before I travel back tomorrow afternoon."

The professor was curious. So, Maddy continued. "Look prof.! Every year after we sign off the performance assessment, I get employees coming up to me with a common complaint: My assessment and rating are incorrect.

Sometimes it is articulated as, 'I have done a lot of good work, contributed to the success of the organisation but neither my feedback nor my rating reflect those contributions.'

Sometimes it is, 'I have done well throughout the year, I would say, not too bad nor anything spectacular but I have been classified as a poor performer. I may not be a star performer but nor am I a poor performer. Why have I been classified under this category?'

At other times, people come and speak similar stuff but about another person, either unfairly given a very good rating or a very bad rating.

Then there are coffee break discussions I have overheard, 'This place has no future. The managers and HR do not know who the right performer is and who is not. They just go by a few incidents here and there and make their perceptions. No one is bothered to check the ground reality. Whoever sucks up to the boss gets a better rating. And if you are just focused on doing your job, don't blame others if you end up with a poor rating'. And stuff like that.

While post-rating frustrations are quite understandable, the reason I am raising it is that I have come to believe there is truth in it. I have observed over and over cases of incorrect ratings, overlooked performances, and judgements gone wrong. It's like the movie 'Shawshank Redemption''; the protagonist is the victim of circumstances and is incarcerated for a crime he didn't commit. Only in these cases, there is no redemption either.

In many cases, the managers accept that they have overlooked some performance cases and made errors in assessment. As a way to recoup the losses, they promise an employee they will take care and overcompensate during the next cycle. However, two wrongs don't make a right; plus, there is no guarantee the employee performance, the manager evaluation, and the final rating, all three will play out as promised the next year. So, all in all, these are empty promises managers make, and employees reject as they try to recover lost ground through job switches. Over the years I have seen this happen time and again and there is no solution I can think of at present. Could you help?"

The professor was sanguine. He said, "Don't be disheartened, Maddy. We are students, students of logic, and human failings, mathematics, and statistics, exact sciences as well as probability, rationality, and irrationality. We haven't found a solution only because we haven't looked in the right places, perhaps. Let's make an attempt tomorrow. For today, let us celebrate what we have achieved."

The professor's words made Maddy feel happy at what they had achieved that day and renewed hope for a brighter tomorrow. Bidding the professor and his wife goodnight, she retired for the night at the campus guesthouse.

CONDITIONAL PROBABILITY & THE DIAGNOSTICS CONUNDRUM

Maddy met the professor for breakfast again. She had packed up for the return trip and checked out of the guesthouse. The professor was chatty during breakfast. He had thought about the question posed by Maddy the night before. He seemed eager to share his understanding.

As soon as they had their tea, he started. "The evolution of business processes over the past century has made computing power the center stage of all decision-making. Computation requires measurement. Measurement requires instruments. And instruments come with their own hit rate/miss rate. This is the basis of the science of *conditional probability: the probability of finding what we are looking for based on the probability of success of the instrument* we use to do the finding itself. You are familiar with conditional probability, aren't you Maddy?" Maddy nodded. The professor continued. "I did some looking up early in the morning on this subject. Frankly, the challenge of finding viable solutions to the problem was at the back of my mind. So, as soon as it was morning, I jumped right into it. Let us examine what I found:

Let us say the probability of a company achieving its target in a financial year is 90%. This would be straight cut, normal probability; no other dependencies here. Now what would be the probability of the same company achieving its target in the same financial year when there is a 90% probability of the market remaining similar to the previous FY. It will be 90% of 90% i.e. 81%.

Uncertainty in the market to the tune of 10% (90% certainty, remember!) reduces the probability of achieving the target by 10% from the previous levels. This is called headwinds in market parlance. This can work in the opposite direction as well, creating tailwinds and giving positive outcomes driven by externalities. How does this work in instruments, both physical and psychometric? Let us see some illustrations.

The loaded dice: In the game of dice, when we roll it a sufficiently large number of times, the chances of obtaining numbers 1, 2, 3, 4, 5 & 6 each are equal or 1/6th (about 17%). Now the dice gets worn out after a large number of rolls. As with getting the numbers, wear and tear is also expected to happen evenly. However, this cannot be guaranteed. If the wear is more on one side, it will affect the rolling leading to unequal distribution in the numbers obtained.

While it looks simple enough when seen from the cause-and-effect angle, life usually follows an effect-and-cause sequence; the effect is observed first and this leads us to investigate and identify the cause, commonly called 'root cause investigation' (RCI). Hence, understanding of conditional probability improves our understanding of physical events and their outcomes."

The professor continued. "The annual health checks are now an established process of getting employees checked for abnormalities and prevent future emergencies. For this reason, they are also termed as 'preventive health checks' by some. ECG is an important part of this diagnostic test battery.

Now, ECG is supposed to read the heart rate and point out the abnormalities, if any, through its report. ECG is pretty accurate at diagnosing many types of heart diseases. Now, how many of us read this and understand that it is pretty accurate at diagnosis, i.e. it is not 100% accurate."

"You are talking in riddles, prof.", Maddy said.

The professor smiled and said, "Let me try again. ECG, as an instrument, has about 90% accuracy in identifying a problematic heart when that heart undergoes an ECG. Sounds very encouraging, right?"

Maddy nodded in affirmative.

"Wrong!" Chuckled the professor. "How?" Asked Maddy, puzzled.

"Well, to start with, not all hearts have a problem (thank god!). It is in fact a small (though increasing) percentage of the population. About 3% of the world's population lives with ischemic heart disease (IHD) at present. With this data, let us get down to analyzing the problem at hand.

1000 people undergo an ECG. 970 people have a healthy heart, and 30 people have IHD; we do not know which 30, so we use an ECG to help us identify. Unfortunately, every instrument comes with its own accuracy rate. We discussed this already; it is 90% for this instrument. So, what do we expect?

We expect 27 out of the 30 'at risk' people to be identified as indeed 'at risk' using this instrument; 3 'at risk' people will get a normal ECG report (unfortunately). This is indeed true. 27 are 'true positive' (the ECG did its intended job) and 3 are 'false negative' (unfortunately).

But the case does not end here. Remember! Cause comes first in only theory, in reality, effect is observed first; cause is deduced from it using investigative techniques. We didn't know which 30 out of the 1000 were 'at risk' before the tests. Hence, we must run all 1000 past the instrument. This is where the confusion (terror, if you are a researcher) starts.

Remember, the instrument continues to have 90% accuracy for all who get tested. That means the 970 'not at risk' population will also receive a 90% accurate report, i.e. 873 of the 970 (90%) will receive a normal ECG ('true negative') but 97 of them will receive an 'at risk' report ('false positive'). Let us look at it in a table:

Employees (Total)	At risk (random) 3%		Not at risk (random) 97%	
1000	30		970	
Instrument accuracy 90%; (Error rate, 10%)	False Negative	True Positive	False Positive	True Negative
Diagnosis	3	27	97	873
What we see (reports)	OK	124 sent for further tests		OK
Accuracy		21% (27 / 124)		NA

What starts off as 90% accurate ends up as 21% accurate with a conditional probability of 3%.

No wonder, modern instruments have increased the doctors' job in shifting through so much false positive data to diagnose those 'at risk'.

This problem will persist, even when the accuracy of the instrument reaches 99%. This is the power of conditional probability.

An illustration will make it clear:

ECG Test subjects (Total)	At risk (random) 3%		Not at risk (random) 97%	
10000	300		9700	
Instrument accuracy 99%; (Error rate 1%)	False Negative	True Positive	False Positive	True Negative
Diagnosis	3	270	97	8730
What we see (reports)	OK	367 sent for further tests		OK
Accuracy		74% (270 / 367)		NA

With an instrument accuracy of 99%, the conditional probability of finding 3% right results is only 74%. While the percentages given here are for illustration only, you would have got the drift, Maddy", said the professor and stopped.

CONDITIONAL PROBABILITY & THE PERFORMANCE CONUNDRUM

It was Maddy's turn to say that psychometric instruments are instruments as much as physical instruments when looked at from the conditional probability angle. The professor agreed.

Maddy continued. "We saw that it is common to have 90% accuracy in physical instruments. Physical measurements use observation by the senses. However, assessment of mental abilities is the realm of perception. So, expecting psychometric instruments to carry somewhat lower accuracy is natural. Here are a few instruments and their estimated accuracy levels:

Instrument (in isolation)	Accuracy (Validity) %
Structured Interview	44%
Unstructured Interview	33%
Biodata / Resume	37%
Years of Work Experience	18%
Educational Pedigree	11%

Different studies have shown the Performance Management System (PMS) to be effective in the range of 50%-80%. By itself, this looks like a very good success rate, in the context of lower levels of validity for selection instruments like interviews. Now let us apply the principle of instrument accuracy, like we did for ECG previously. How well does it do its job? Let us take 80% as the best-case scenario i.e. the PMS is 80% accurate in identifying the right performance level."

The professor now stepped in. He said, "Let us now look at the spread of performance in a population, much like finding the 3% persons with heart problem. However, here we have not one but two variations to identify using the same instrument:

The PMS must identify the 'above average' performers from among the 'average' lot.

It must identify the 'below average' performers from among the 'average' lot as well.

This gives us an additional dimension to deal with. It is like an ECG that can identify a weaker-than-normal heart and a stronger-than-normal heart as well. Hope, the employees know what the expectations from the HR instruments are. Even the doctors will not envy the HR folks for this. Anyway, here are the illustrations of the conditional probability.

Employees Performance	Below Average 10%		Average 80%			Above Average 10%	
Sample size, 1000	100		800			100	
Results at 80% accuracy	80	20	80	640	80	20	80
PMS Class*	TP	FN	FN-Tail1	TP	FN-Tail2	FN	TP
PMS Descriptor	Below Average	Average	Below Average	Average	Above Average	Average	Above Average

*TP: True Positive; FN: False Negative

But remember, life usually follows an effect-and-cause sequence i.e. the effect is observed first. Let's look at how the effect looks:

CATCHING CHIMERA

Employees Performance Class	Below Average		Average			Above Average	
Estimated %	10%		80%			10%	
Sample size, 1000	100		800			100	
Results at 80% accuracy	80	80	20	640	20	80	80
PMS Class*	TP	FN-Tail1	FN	TP	FN	FN-Tail2	TP
Classification	Below Average	Below Average	Average	Average	Average	Above Average	Above Average
Class Count	160		680			160	
Accuracy	50% (80 / 160)		94% (640/680)			50% (80/160)	
Revised class %	16% (up from 10%)		68% (down from 80%)			16% (up from 10%)	

*TP: True Positive; FN: False Negative

As we observe, the classes have moved from 10%-80%-10% to 16%-68%-16% kind of ranges due to the interaction of conditional probability. From here, even if HR and business decide to force the distribution back to 10%-80%-10% spread, the accuracy will remain the same. This is because 16% of the population on either side is already at 50% accuracy. So, moving 160 on either side down to 100 people will move 60 random people each into the middle (average) class, leaving the accuracy unchanged at 50%.

So, what was the purpose with which we started the PMS? To identify the two tails (non-average performers). What was our instrument's accuracy? 80%. What success did we end up with? 50% success rate on either side.

50% of the identified stars are not stars.
50% of the identified poor performers are not poor performers at all.
However, 94% of the identified average performers are indeed so.

Even in the best-case scenario, the system is great at finding average performers but is terrible at finding stars and laggards. No wonder, employee feedback on PMS is 50-50. It is far more accurate than most of us realize."

Maddy was aghast looking at the numbers and percentages. She realized the gravity of the situation.

LIVE, DIE, REPEAT
EDGE OF TOMORROW

The professor was on a roll. "The traditional system, as we observed, routinely throws 50% of the star performers under the bus, terming them as 'average'. What is worse, it simultaneously elevates an equal number of average performers into the 'star' category rubbing salt on injury.

The scene is equally bad at the other end as well; 50% of the poor performers escape the reprimand, and a chance to improve by getting branded as 'average'. This reduces the meaning of 'average' itself. Along with this, the system throws an equal number of 'average' poor devils under the bus of 'performance improvement plan' (PIP) by tagging them as 'below average'.

You were speaking of post-appraisal rants at the coffee place about what a convoluted, incorrect performance appraisal someone had received. And the same guys would wonder how some poor 'below average' bloke escaped the axe, landing a decent merit increase. I hope it makes sense now.

Over time we have come to label some who succeed as 'chamcha' (henchman) who suck up to the bosses. Even so, it is confounding to see only a few of these succeed. The bosses seem helpless in giving a good appraisal to all those 'deserving' in their eyes. If so, blame it on the 'conditional probability'.

So, what are the factors we are working with, in this problem, Maddy?"

Maddy recounted them:
1. Bell Curve: The condition that there are three segments of performers, about 10% below average performers, about 10% above average performers, and 80% 'at par' performers.
2. Instrument Error: The accuracy rate of the appraisal process in doing a correct identification of each segment is 80% at best.

The professor observed, "The instrument accuracy is pretty static, derived from multiple iterations and observations. The performance classes are also pretty predictable, derived from multiple iterations over multiple locations, businesses, and time intervals. So, both are pretty inflexible in their capacity to influence the outcome. But what if the outcome itself is turned into a variable!

Let me elaborate; the outcome is derived by running the instrument over the population only once (presumably at the end of the assessment period). While we cannot eliminate the error generated during the measurement, can we repeat the measurement? What happens when we repeat the measurement? We bring in the element of frequency, and that can possibly turn the table in our favour."

Maddy felt excited hearing this.

"Let me narrate to you the plot of this movie I saw sometime back", said the professor. "The movie 'Live Die Repeat, Edge of Tomorrow' is a sci-fi adventure. In this movie, the Earth is attacked by an alien species wanting to eliminate the human race and colonize the planet. They have a real possibility of doing so, because of a special power they possess; the power to be reborn at the same time they die. This helps them to be reborn every time they die in battle. Humans of course cannot do this; so, the world comes to the verge of human extinction.

Just about this time, the protagonists discover that they are able to gain the same power of rebirth when, by a stroke of luck, they get drenched in one of the aliens' blood. From here on, the story goes: the protagonist goes to the battlefield, gets killed, gets reborn, goes back to the battle but this time moving a little further, and getting killed a little further than before. The movie ends when he is born again, one last time and is able to reach the place where the alpha alien resides, is able to kill it, and save the human race.

As I connect this story to our current topic, if only we could keep making attempts to measure the performance of the employees more often than once, every iteration will add some more data and help us get a better understanding of the performance of the individual. This will aid us in making less and less error i.e. the accuracy of the instrument will remain unchanged but frequent use of the instrument will reduce the error rate. Let us see how.

When the performance is measured once, we get the following distribution:

Probability of Distribution	Employees Performance Class	Below Average		Average			Above Average	
Condition1	Estimated %	10%		80%			10%	
	Sample size: 1000	100		800			100	
Condition2	PMS Instrument Accuracy: 80%	80% TP	20% FN	10% FN-Tail1	80% TP	10% FN-Tail2	20% FN	80% TP
	PMS Class*	80 BA (True)	20 Avg (False)	80 BA (False)	640 Avg (True)	80 AA (False)	20 Avg (False)	80 AA (True)
Conditional Probability (Applied)	Class Count	160		680			160	
	Classification	Below Average		Average			Above Average	
	Accuracy	50% (80 / 160)		94% (640/680)			50% (80/160)	
	Revised class %	16%		68% (down from 80%)			16%	
Bell Curve Normalization	Revised Class (Accuracy)	100 (only 50 are truly below avg.)		800 (700 are truly avg., 50 below avg. & 50 above avg. incorrectly classified as avg.)			100 (only 50 are truly above avg.)	

*TP: True Positive; FN: False Negative; BA: Below Average; AA: Above Average

Half the 'below average' performers do not truly belong to that class. So how do they land there? Well, they land there because they perform poorly during that moment of measurement. In a roll of dice, getting a '6' score has a probability of about 17% (1/6th) if repeated often enough. But if we roll it just once, and get a '1' score, what would you call it? Tough luck!

Think of our performer similarly: He has his good days and bad days. If he were an average performer, he would do well about half the time and poorly the other half, provided we observe often enough. If observed only once, he will be classified based on how he performs on the day of performance measurement.

10% chance: He doesn't do well, tough luck and a false negative (tail1) from the data gatherer (instrument); he will be classified as a poor performer.

80% chance: He does an average job, a true positive from the data gatherer (instrument); he will be classified as an average performer.

10% chance: He does very well, again a false positive (this time tail2) from the data gatherer (instrument); he will be classified as a star performer. Now let us repeat this once more. What happens to the probability now?

Probability of Distribution: Two Observations		Employee Performance Class	Below Avg.				Average				Above Avg.	
Conditional Probability, 1st Pass*	1	Dist. %	10%				80%				10%	
	2	Instrument Accuracy: 80%	8% BA (T)		2% Avg (F)		8% BA (F)	64% Avg (T)		8% AA (F)	2% Avg (F)	8% AA (T)
Conditional Probability, 2nd Pass*	1	Dist.%	80%	20%	80%	20%	80%	20%				
	2	Instrument Accuracy: 80%	6.4% T-T	1.6% T-F	1.6% F-T	0.4% F-F	6.4% F-F	1.6% F-T				
Outcome %			8% Below Avg. (True) + 6.4% Below Avg. (False)									
Accuracy % at Two Observations for Below Avg. Performance Class			56% (8% from 14.4%)									

* BA: Below Average; AA: Above Average; T-T: True-True; T-F: True-False; F-T: False-True; F-F: False-False

As we can see, the chances of finding a 'poor performer' in the 'below average' rating class is 50% if done once; however, it improves to 56% when repeated just once more.

This means, the more we iterate the assessment, the more the probability is of doing an accurate job and reducing the instrument error.

So how many times should we iterate the performance measurement? Every six months, every 3 months, or every month? Let us experiment.

Iteration	True Rate (either leg. Below Avg. or Above Avg.)	False Rate	% of Population	% Accuracy
1	8%	8%	16.0%	50%
2	8%	6.4%	14.4%	56%
3	8%	5.1%	13.1%	61%
4	8%	4.1%	12.1%	66%
5	8%	3.3%	11.3%	71%
6	8%	2.6%	10.6%	75%
7	8%	2.1%	10.1%	79%
8	8%	1.7%	9.7%	83%
9	8%	1.3%	9.3%	86%
10	8%	1.1%	9.1%	88%
11	8%	0.9%	8.9%	90%
12	8%	0.7%	8.7%	92%

So, you see Maddy! We can wallow in self-pity and continue to blame the instrument's limitations - they are not going to go away, or we beat this conditional probability with a higher frequency of observations and decrease the error rate."

Maddy got up from her seat and did a kowtow to the professor. She was genuinely impressed with the professor's ability to connect the dots. The professor on his part was jubilant at finding practical use for his protégé.

With this, Maddy bade goodbye to the professor and hurried to the airport for the travel back to home base. She was excited. She was ready!

PART IV: CHIMERA

AN IDEA
WHOSE TIME HAS COME

The discussion with the CEO went well. He had vented his frustration that day and had forgotten about it. He didn't expect Maddy to go and find a solution to the problem. He appreciated this go-getter attitude. He suggested Maddy get the other CxOs onboard before the rollout. He could hear the money clanking, what with the savings and sharp business focus that this change would usher in. But Maddy was not sure the R&D head would agree that easily. Yet that was the first port of call. It was the smaller of the SBUs in terms of headcount. It was also the place with a scientists' community. Maddy estimated appealing to the logico-rational brains of the R&D guys had a better chance at success for this kind of scientific overhaul of the system.

The R&D, as an SBU was less predictable than operations and had a longer-term outcome focus than the sales, a unique challenge to say the least. Archana, the R&D head was known to be a highly accomplished scientist and a leader with keen business sense. This rare combination had propelled her to the SBU head role at an age most scientists would get to lead a team at best. She was leading the research efforts of the entire company and was on the boards of several scientific advisory committees as well.

Among friends, she was known as a keen observer of data and a student of logic. To her adversaries, she was known as the Ice Queen, cold, calculative, business savvy and unforgiving to errors. In board meetings, she would argue why R&D cannot be held to a monthly deadline like sales with such polish that even the CBO would not venture to dispute it. At the next meeting, she could complete with operations to demand that the operations head accommodate her new product launches citing the disproportionate profit that the new product launches would bring vis-a-vis the running products. The operations head would protest that this would disturb the set monthly batch planning but to no avail. The CEO and the CFO could not but side with her much to the chagrin of the COO. The CBO and the COO both hated her charm, her guts, her business acumen and her scientific competence but they couldn't help but admire her for all the same things as well.

That is why Maddy felt trepidation walking into the pitch. She met her at the R&D centre.

Maddy: Hi Archana, how do you do? How is work coming along?

Archana: Not bad, Maddy!

Maddy: How do you monitor the performance of your team at regular intervals, doc?

Archana: Well, I have a competent set of scientists who know their job. I set goals in the beginning and monitor them at regular intervals. I think the results have been good. I don't need much tinkering around at present.

The first attempt was off the mark! Maddy was worried now. She pressed on, nonetheless.

Maddy: What is your team size?

Archana: You are the HR head. You must know this. Anyway, I have a team of about 450 scientists / engineers. They work in three verticals viz. molecular research, analytical research and technology transfer. There are about 150 researchers, 250 analytical development scientists and the remaining technology transfer experts led by an able 'vice president and head of function' in each area. The function heads in turn report to me. Each of them interfaces with business lines facing different market clusters and collaborates with colleagues from across these verticals for know-how exchange and market access. This helps us bring relevant products to the market in the shortest possible time. But this you already know.

Maddy: So, how frequently do we evaluate this large a team?

Archana: Why, annually of course.

Maddy: How do they get rated?

Archana: You are asking things I had asked you during my joining and induction. What's going on?

Maddy: Humour me, Doc. How do they get rated?

Archana: OK, they get rated on a three-point scale, 'not met', 'met', and 'met and exceeded' their goals.

Maddy: Your scientists must be satisfied with the current system, right?

Archana: Yes, we give '0', '1' or '2' for each goal. There are about 5 to 6 goals for each scientist. The weighted average outcome of all 5-6 goals is the score for the scientist for the year.

Sample		Employee 1		Employee 2		Employee 3	
Goal	Weight	Perf. (0-1-2)	Wt. Score	Perf. (0-1-2)	Wt. Score	Perf. (0-1-2)	Wt. Score
#1	30%	1	30%	1	30%	1	30%
#2	10%	0	0%	1	10%	2	20%
#3	25%	2	50%	1	25%	1	25%
#4	15%	1	15%	0	0%	1	15%
#5	20%	0	0%	1	20%	1	20%
Total	100%	NA	95%	NA	85%	NA	110%
Result		At Par		Below Par		Above Par	

Maddy: Managers give reasons for giving 0-1-2, right?

Archana: Well, they discuss the reasons with the scientists.

Maddy: When the managers give '0' on a goal, does it mean the goal is not achieved?

Archana: No, it is more like 60-70% completion. My managers are aware of the consequences of unfinished work and do a good job of giving the right feedback.

Maddy: Do the scientists / managers not make errors of judgement?

Archana: Yes, of course. But we are scientists, we keep a sharp eye out for error percentage. For instance, the purity of a medicine we make cannot be less than 99.4%. What's more, we have a detailed list of what can constitute the remaining 0.6% as well. It's called an impurity profile. Any deviation from these standards and the batch is rejected. But you wouldn't know, HR is not that accurate.

Ouch! Maddy felt like reacting but held her calm and prodded on.

Maddy: I agree Doc. It's not this accurate and you know why as well. The batch rejection you spoke about, though not frequent, is not unheard of. And that happens because of those who run the batch. The chemicals would not even come in contact with each other but for us humans. And humans are not machines; we make errors far in excess of 0.6%, won't you agree?

Archana: Ya, on that point you have my sympathy. I like working with mathematical precision. I get upset when I see avoidable errors borne out of sheer carelessness. And when done by astute scientists, I don't know what to say. Believe me, they are not that uncommon. Makes me think that yours must be a tough job working with imprecise human outcomes. I guess HR is more of an art than a science.

Maddy: Hold on, Doc. Just because humans don't behave with the mathematical precision of machines doesn't mean that the subject of humans can't be dealt with as a science. In fact, all large-scale interdependent ecosystems work on the complexity of thousands of possible outcomes. The way to work with such complexity is to a) create models with estimates that a particular outcome may happen with a certain level of certainty, called the study of probability and b) repeat small-scale experiments with representative data and use empirical repetitive outcomes as possible solutions, called the study of statistics.

Probability and statistics are the best friends of human data analysis. You must have heard about exit poll surveys of elections, the most famous users of statistics to analyse large-scale human behaviour. Don't you love watching the dramatic style in which psephologists present their predictions? That's hypothesis testing in statistics. They get it right many times and they go wrong now and then as well. That's because either the samples turn out not to be representative or the responders decide to actively corrupt the data input, i.e. they decide to do something (vote) and say something else (during the survey). Welcome to the world of humans!

And they both had a hearty laugh.

Archana: Okay, you had me there. You have a tough job! As tough as mine. But I haven't seen an HR guy using probability and statistics for scientific outcomes in their day-to-day jobs. My most memorable HR recall is brilliant annual celebration nights and messy annual performance appraisals involving half-baked unscientific tools like forced distribution that you HR folks call 'Bell Curve'.

Maddy: On that point, how would you like a performance management system without a bell curve that still passes the board approval!

Archana: Is it possible? I would like to know, Maddy. Let's meet next week and discuss this in detail.

Maddy: OK, done.

Maddy was pleased with herself. Well begun was half done.

***

They met the next week as planned.

Archana: Hey girl! What's up? You know, you got me hooked the last time we spoke. I couldn't stop thinking, about how human data is used in everyday situations using probability and statistics. Come to think of it, the sales, marketing and advertising folks are almost entirely dependent on the analysis of human behaviour. The sales guys use market segmentation to bring sales focus. Marketing folks use consumer behaviour data to create, implement and monitor greater bang for their buck. The advertising industry is entirely driven by human psychology.

Heck! Even the boring predictable finance people are using behavioural finance as the cutting-edge tool to work the stock markets. "Irrational behaviour" is the cornerstone of several business fields. I am sure all of this involves a heavy dose of probability and statistics. Then why can't the HR guys use the same to work on processes that are 100% human-centric; makes eminent sense. Only one question remains: why you people haven't used them till now? Wait! Don't answer it. Tell me instead, how are you planning on using it? Let's see that.

Maddy: Wow, Archana. I couldn't have thought of a better take-off pitch. Now that we have, let's get down to the brass tacks.

And Maddy explained to Archana the concept of conditional probability, the diagnostic conundrum and the performance conundrum as well.

Archana: I am floored. It is so frustrating to do performance appraisals every year in my large team and lose good guys despite my best efforts in giving them a fair evaluation. I finally get it. The system is just not geared to do this job. It's like looking at a movie poster and guessing the storyline. One is not going to be very successful at that. But in the case of the PMS, when we fail to predict the story from the poster, we blame the producer for making a poor poster and more blame game follows, not solutions. Go on, tell me what's the way out.

Maddy: We repeat the measurement every month.

Archana: But it will be very time-consuming. Remember! We have about 450 team members. And you HR folks have to get the entire company's evaluation done. You people yourselves take about two months to complete the annual process. So doing it every month is definitely not a good solution. I am reminded of Heisenberg's uncertainty principle. If we try and measure the location of a moving particle at an atomic level, we will not be able to measure its speed. On the other hand, measurement of speed will make location measurement impossible. I am worried that trying to measure performance will take up so much time that no time will be left to perform. How do you overcome this dilemma?

Maddy: Well! Complex problems do not always need complex solutions; most of the difficult problems have been solved using rather simple solutions. Remember the problem of astronauts not being able to use pens in space due to lack of gravity? And some solved this by simply using pencils! An elegant solution to a complex problem, found by going to the root of it. These solutions might look simple even rather stupid in hindsight but are worth their weight in gold on an RoI scale.

Archana: So, what's our pencil pointer here?

Maddy: We don't evaluate 80% of the population, during the monthly review, at all.

Archana: Oh, come on! The answer to 'how to evaluate' cannot be 'do not evaluate'. What's the trick here?

Maddy: What are the smallest and largest teams your managers handle?

Archana: The smallest can be just a one-person team. This would be a short-term situation though. The largest team of scientists are in the laboratories with 8 to 10 of them working on analytical techniques. There are times when there is a senior scientist vacancy, a colleague may be required to handle an additional team for a while, something like a 20-member team; a less frequent but not unusual situation.

Maddy: Okay! Evaluating 20 team members is indeed a tall ask. Let's look at it. There are goals for each team member. So, they are expected to complete their job as per the targets given, right?

Archana: Right.

Maddy: So, what's the usual scenario? How many people in your team do their job as per expectations? I mean, what's the percentage of average Joe's in your team?

Archana: About 80%. The spread of high-average-low performance is 10%-80%-10%, isn't it?

Maddy: That's about 16 out of 20 people in the example of the largest team possible, right?

Archana: Right. We know this. That still leaves us with the job of identifying those 16 out of 20 people, isn't it? How do we NOT evaluate and yet know who they are?

Maddy: Sure, let's try with your experience of dealing with your direct reports and see if that can be replicated at scale.

Archana: Okay.

Maddy: You have 5 direct reports, isn't it?

Archana: Yes. 3 Vice Presidents and 2 Directors. The Directors are both SMEs.

Maddy: What do you remember of their work in the last 30 days? Let's start with the top-of-the-mind recall.

Archana: I remember pulling one guy up for a shoddy

outcome.

Maddy: Okay, what else? Who else?

Archana: Hmm! Let me see (thinking hard). Wait, this other guy got us a breakthrough in the research technique. While there is no immediate impact on results it will give us an edge over others in the speed to market.

Maddy: You see! We are programmed to recall the negatives faster than the positives. You did recall the positive as well, after some effort. What else?

Archana: (thinking some more) Sorry, I can't recall anything more, neither that good nor that bad that would warrant a strong memory.

Maddy: Okay! So, here is the thumb rule to use for a manager in a monthly performance review: give a zero if you recall something that gave you poor results. Give a two if you recall a success or a positive outcome. Now, the magic rule: *give a 'one' score to all others, the silent 80% majority* (in your direct reports' case, 60%).

The paradigm shift is this: if you cannot recall anything done by a person during a time period (and you have no other parameter of measurement), most probably s/he was doing her/his job during that time. Imagine the nuisance it would be if all the 80% of the silent majority chose to tom-tom their work every day! It would be an everyday headache for the manager.

So, let's remember: *if we can't recall someone's work, it is NOT bad; it means s/he is doing her/his job. Let's give this lot the one score.*

See! We rated all of your team in about 10 minutes for

last month's performance. The real deal would be a little more elaborate than the 'back of the paper' scoring we did just now but the results wouldn't be that different. The extra time spent in preparing the ratings would pay off in enhancing the quality of feedback with each of your direct reports. Even that interaction need not be more than 15 minutes a month per person. This is how we can handle performance ratings and feedback for a team of anything between 1 and 20 members. What do you think?

Archana: I think I love HR!

And they both laugh out loud.

THE NEW BEGINNING

Maddy met and updated the CEO about what transpired between her and the R&D Head. He expected Maddy to succeed, dogged pursuer that she was. And yet, he couldn't help but be impressed by Maddy's communication skills. Still, the system couldn't be rolled out without the COO and Quality Head coming on board. Maddy got down to work. It took her the next two weeks and four sittings with them. Both were worried the operations people would not welcome it. They were used to the annual assessment process. Maddy knew the psychological archetype of each function only too well.

The R&D scientists and researchers were required to work on innovation and process improvement on a daily basis. So, they were not averse to change.

The operations executives were required to adhere to the SOPs (standard operating procedures) by the work requirement. Deviations from standards meant failure. So, they looked at any deviation from the routine with suspicion.

The customer-facing role holders in commercial / business development were used to drastic variations in targets and achievements. Failure and rejection were routine phenomena requiring them to develop a thick skin to absorb such daily barrage. They took change in their stride. So, by job design,

Commercial employees are highly flexible but low on following procedures.
Operations employees are highly inflexible but high on following procedures and,
Research and development employees are somewhat flexible and somewhat process-oriented.

With this in mind, she approached the COO and the Quality Head with the process gaps, the proposed changes and the benefits.

Change from routine is looked at with suspicion by the operations folks because it is classified as deviation. What happens when a deviation is analysed and found to be intrinsic to the process requirement! It does happen now and then in manufacturing that a new raw material is introduced. This changes the analysis limits. If the SOPs are not upgraded to incorporate the new limits, the output will have to be recorded as a deviation. To incorporate this variation, operations and quality teams come together to initiate a process called, 'change control'. Using this change control protocol, the SOPs are upgraded, limits modified, tested, validated and revised SOPs given to users for routine operations from thereon.

Maddy was familiar with this process of managing change. When in Rome, be a Roman. She followed this process to introduce the new performance management system as a necessary change control. The COO was on board.

With the Quality Head, she pitched the new system as a necessary upgrade to the existing system to stay contemporaneous. Contemporaneous is one of the elements of ALCOA principles, the cornerstone of pharmaceutical quality assurance. ALCOA is a framework for data management. All data generated by the industry must be Attributable, Legible, Contemporaneous, Original and Accurate. Over time, more elements have been added to make it more comprehensive. No quality professional could say no to ALCOA principles. The dye was cast.

The new performance management system was launched as a low-key affair. Maddy did not want to go overboard or become overconfident. She wanted people to come along and be part of the experiment. She and her team conducted roadshows in each of the locations ending with the corporate headquarters. The rollout happened as per plan.

WIN-WIN

The new performance management system took root in its own way. Each CxO, each site leader, each function leader, and each employee experienced it up close and personal as a user. They experienced it as employees, L1 managers, L2 managers, HR, and many other role holders.

Each month gave rise to something interesting. Maddy and her team made every attempt to address the issues, resolve the glitches and sign off the scores. They conducted frequent roadshows and townhalls to familiarise the users with the nuances of the new system. Maddy was firm in her communication: this is a new system and new systems come with a built-in gap; they are untested, so there can be bugs – process gaps that have gone unnoticed. So, nothing was to be considered as unquestionable. Everything could be examined, questioned, verified and only when thoroughly satisfied, implemented. As and when improvements were found, it was to be welcomed not dismissed as extra work. Maddy stayed in touch with the professor to exchange notes, take advice, provide updates and share stories of success and failure.

The collective improvement approach allowed the people to embrace the new system with less suspicion. And it showed in the month-on-month progress in becoming more and more acceptable. And before Maddy realised, the year was up.

It was time to analyse the scores and use them to decide annual merit increases. The outcome of 12 months' usage had already thrown up a range of scores between 8 and 16, with 12 as the median. The performance for the year for the company had been concluded at 85% so getting a distribution with a tilt towards poorer than median rating was the expected thing to do. Ideally, the weighted average of all ratings should have been 10.2 (85%). However, in practice, L1 managers were more compassionate while rating very poor performers and more conservative while rating very high performers. Statisticians called it 'central tendency bias'. So, the rating distribution was expected to have a lower spread compared to business performance distribution, if observed over multiple periods. Both these illustrations follow.

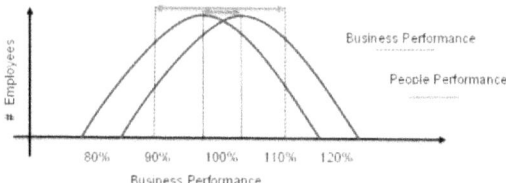

The previous system was less aggressive both in rewarding as well as disincentivizing the two sides of performance respectively. By bringing in greater detail, more data and focus, business was expected to get more out of the doers and see the laggards more clearly. Thus, the ultimate winner in this new scheme were both employees (the contributors) and the organization.

MODUS VIVENDI

It was PMS closing time, with only the final review by the leadership team remaining. Maddy had published the rules well in advance that there was to be no annual rating. The annual leg of the new system was a time for doing self-assessment and receiving long-term feedback.

This process involved giving a) self-assessment by the employee, b) annual review and feedback by L1 manager, c) an opportunity for L2 manager to validate the L1 manager's feedback, d) receipt of annual rating that was the sum-total of all monthly ratings and e) acknowledgement by the employee. The R&D Head, the COO, the Head of Quality and the CBO were like the bulwark against any deviation in the monthly performance review process. Maddy was pleased to have had such strong sponsors for a people's program.

At last, they reached the final stage in the process. One more nudge and Maddy knew they would have demonstrated a complete cycle of this new system. Maddy got down to the task at hand in earnest. The stages of self-assessment by employees, the first stage, were rolled out. Within a week it was time for L1 managers to give feedback and in another week, it was the for the L2 manager to complete their feedback and review. When it was time to upload the ratings, Maddy consulted the CXOs if all the ratings were okay to be published. Did anyone want to use the option of leadership review to have a re-look at any of the sum-total ratings? The Quality Head and the COO each were very strict with their own category heads and site heads respectively. They had been true to the principles of '0' for anything less than 90% achievement and '2' for anything more than 100% achievement. This had landed the 4 category heads and site heads in scores of 6, 6, 7, 9 and 6, 6, 7, 8 (out of max. 12) respectively. This meant the category heads and site heads had received ~7 out of 12 (58%) performance score. This was below the company-level average employee median score of 11 (~92%). On the other hand, the rest of the CXOs had been practical in going with more ones and an occasional two, keeping the overall people performance scores (~92%) in mind more than the exact performance of the site (85%). Which was the right approach?

Maddy, the HR head was pragmatic. She believed in the tenet 'few truths in life are universal, the rest are more likely statistically significant'.

The truth was that the site performance score and employee aggregate score confirmed that employee ratings at the macro level were more liberal than they should have been.

However, what was more interesting was the inconsistency of the positive bias across businesses and operating sites. In any case, correcting the liberal bias was easier said than done.

Remember the hypothesis that while business scores tend to swing from very low (70%) to very high (130%) levels, the people who bring in these business scores are evaluated with 'central tendency bias'. The bosses usually are not too harsh when the going is bad. They understand that the results turn bad many times due to externalities and discount this away. They also understand that extraordinary performances are also caused due to externalities in many cases as well. Therefore, they give moderately high 'performance' ratings during very good performance periods. Notable exceptions could be the frontline salespersons. Their performance ratings are completely dependent on a more straightforward mathematical outcome of results.

So, coming back to the stance of pragmatism, Maddy believed the harsh ratings of category heads and site heads should be brought in line with the median score. That would be a more practical option than aligning the entire organization's people performance download to match the category head / site head's harsh ratings. While the latter was the right way, it was not the practical way. How would it look if all ratings were revised downwards? That would bring the entire evaluation process and the competence of the managers in evaluating their team into question. This would lead to the entire system and process being discredited.

But the Quality Head and the COO would have none of this. They said they did as fair an evaluation as could be done. Why should they revise that now? Maddy knew they were right, but they were in the statistical minority. So how do we break the deadlock? Maddy was in a fix. She let herself sleep over the issue.

Two weeks passed with no signs of a thaw. Then came the week when the CEO told her he had the approval of the NRC to go ahead with merit increases and the annual bonuses. The groundwork for merit-increase grid was completed following the standard practice. The market had indicated about 10% year on year increase. That being the median, percentage increases were drawn up for higher and lower than median score to complete the merit increase grid for the year.

The COO and the Quality Head along with other CxOs confabulated and proposed disproportionate increases and decreases for those with current compensations that were off their respective median compensation. When the CEO reviewed this, he asked for the budget usage. It was at 100%. He was upset. He asked the CxOs how they expected him to approach the NRC with the proposal to pay 100% of the budget at 85% of goal achievement! It had to be brought closer to the top-down number. His guidance was to bring it to 90% and the NRC might just let it be approved. So, the revised version was finally prepared with much higher punishment and rewards on both sides of the median. A full percentage point of the budget was saved. The leadership felt this would send the right message to the employees.

Now came the problem statement: the ratings of those 8 category heads and site heads. Their on-ground performances were hardly any different from those of their peers, but their performance scores were way below their peers' scores. This was the opportunity Maddy was waiting for. When the Quality Head and the COO were confronted with this reality they had no choice but to pull the scores of their direct reports up. 6, 6, 7, 9 & 6, 6, 7, 8 became 10, 10, 11, 13 & 10, 10, 11, 12 i.e. on the average ~11 out of 12 (~92%). The category heads and the site heads were now going to get compensation raises in line with the company average merit increase. A disaster was averted skilfully.

PART V: THE EVER AFTER

INSTANT KARMA

Maddy and her team reaped the benefits of this new way of working over the next few years. While the new performance management system served the purpose for which it was primarily created, it gave rise to some unplanned, unintended aftereffects as well.

It was the second month of implementation. The month-on-month performance management system had taken the baby step of finishing the first month, the first run. It was a surreal feeling for the managers and employees alike. Some had got tough feedback and a '0' rating. Some had a pleasant surprise of getting a '2' score. Most had received a 'results as expected' i.e. '1' rating. The cafeteria at lunchtime was abuzz with performance discussion. Everyone was asking everyone else, what rating they got. It was liberating for many to know that they could discuss each other's ratings freely, a very strange departure from the past when it was forbidden to share one's own rating as well as ask someone else's. Some of the '0' scorers had skipped the lunchtime cafeteria crowd, unwilling to discuss their scores further. Those who had scored a '2' were acting like celebrities, giving out free advice on how to ace the scores. They had to face some sceptics as well who wouldn't accept their scores as justified. Overall, there was a sense of jubilation that something new had happened in HR in a long time. The HR guys for once were being mobbed with queries, not complaints, on how this process worked, what were the consequences, whether it was possible to reverse the scores, how to appeal a re-evaluation and many more.

Maddy gathered her team and asked them how it felt. There was a general murmur of agreement and smiles all around. None of them had received a '2' score but none had a '0' score as well. They seemed happy at watching an innovation take root in HR in a long time. One was bold enough to state that he didn't believe it would take off. He was happy he was proven wrong. Maddy nodded in agreement. She was not beholden to running this process at any cost, no. She wanted to experiment with this new way of working as much as the users themselves. She didn't want to fall in love with her own creation like Pygmalion. But she need not have worried; the system seemed error-free and idiot-proof. Mentally, she thanked the professor every time she observed the simple yet elegant processes that they had co-created.

It was time for the next step in the series of elegant steps. Maddy asked the Site HR Heads how they were conducting their 'Employee of the Month' engagement programs. She knew it of course; she wanted them to describe it to her. The engagement program was part of the periodic 'reward and recognition' (R&R) initiatives HR used to conduct. All the employees at a site were requested to upload what they saw as 'good work' by fellow employees. These were considered as nominations. One could not file a self-nomination. So, colleagues and managers used to upload other's nominations on the online R&R page. Most of it was prepared by the employees themselves and passed on to others for upload. This was an open secret. At the end of the month, all the nominations were evaluated by a team of cross-functional SMEs. The experts chose one nomination as the 'Employee of the Month'. There were some consolation awards for those who missed by a few counts in the eyes of the jury. They were given certificates much like the Oscars gave out 'nominee' and 'winner' lists.

Maddy asked her team what they think should now be done to sync the existing practice with the new rating process. The R&R was a good platform, and good platforms were not to be treated lightly. On the other hand, there were no performance scores previously, so the nominations were the only way to identify the good performers. She accepted that the employees had figured out a way to game the system and secure a nomination. The program had lost some of the sheen now. It was a pain securing sufficient nominations. It was a struggle getting the jury to meet and sign off the winner. Employees had started saying only HR was interested in the R&R and that too as a check box activity. Her team agreed with the narrative. They were the most affected by this lack of support from the site. An interesting program had turned into a thankless job for HR over time.

Maddy asked again, "What should we do to sync the existing practice with the new rating process? And in the process, if we can revive the interest of employees in R&R, it would be icing on the cake". It was the US Site HR Lead who gave the idea:

Why not use the performance scores as nominations! All the '2' score holders could be automatically nominated to the 'Employee of the Month' shortlist. No need to ask people to fill out nomination forms, create a process for upload, and examine the case contents, none of this was necessary anymore. The L1 managers who were giving '2' scores were also giving feedback and details of 'above par' results. That could easily form the basis for nominations. In fact, these scores had come post review by the site leadership and endorsement by the company, much like the nomination process, only now not just for R&R but for multiple uses. Also, previously the nominations could come for 'average' performances as well. It was the duty of the jury to shift through all that data remove such cases. With the rating system being monthly, allowing only the '2' scorers was now automatic. And, as the site leadership was signing off the monthly rating, the same meeting could be extended by some more time to find who among the '2' scores should be the 'Employee of the Month'.

All '2' scores were 'above par' performers, they deserved to be felicitated with a certificate of recognition. And one among them could be chosen to be the 'Employee of the Month' a more equal among the equals.

The idea seemed to remove an entire set of time-consuming activities like nominations and selections and replace them with an effective, scientific and acceptable solution that could be done effortlessly by staying in sync with the performance management process. Maddy's team was excited. In a long time, they were seeing an activity getting dropped off their bucket list without lowering the effectiveness of program delivery, in fact enhancing it. They were all charged up to go and implement it.

While moving out someone commented, this was like instant karma. You do well in a month, and before the next month is out, you get your rating, you get your feedback and god willing, you get your 'Employee of the Month' reward; time lapses like 'waiting for the year to end' was a thing of the past.

DAWN OF REALITY

It was morning 10 o'clock and unusual for Jagan to have called. Jagan was the HR Lead for one of the operating sites. Maddy picked it up and immediately got the vibe that he was upset about something. Before Maddy could ask he revealed the cause as well. He had seen his rating given by Maddy. He started asking Maddy right away, the reason he had been given a '0' rating.

Maddy knew this was coming but she didn't expect it so soon. However, now that it had, Maddy quickly gathered her thoughts and asked, "Jagan, the ratings are yet to be published. Because you have the admin access as HR, you are able to see the scores proposed by the L1 managers. And it happens to include your score as well. Would you wish the scores to be published first and then we do a formal discussion, or do you wish to discuss it right away knowing that this will be the final score, let me know."

Pat came the response, "I wish to discuss right away. I believe the scores will be accepted by the L2 manager as well. In any case, I know your opinion of my performance for the month now and I do not agree with it."

Maddy knew from working with Jagan that he was not a person to hold back. Even then, she felt uncomfortable upon hearing Jagan's blunt opinion. As the process owner and as HR herself, Maddy could not take the "boss is always right" route. That would fly in the face of what she believed in fervently i.e. managers have a duty to make their team members understand the evaluation process. They must not only explain it but also ensure the team member accepts it voluntarily. In the absence of the same, it's no different from "my way or highway". Besides, the basic premise of "giving feedback to ensure improvement" won't happen without acceptance of feedback. And an unconvinced employee is like a 'bull in a China shop'. Will they stay silent but become non-cooperative and non-productive, or badmouth the manager, or badmouth the process or the entire system, or the company, where will they stop? It will depend on their feeling of being incorrectly assessed and their feeling of hurt. Add to this the fact that the employee is the HR Lead himself and your deadly concoction is ready to go out and cause damage.

So, Maddy started by asking him to explain the reasons he didn't agree with the assessment. Jagan said he had done all the work assigned to him that month. There's been no lapse. So, he couldn't figure out why he was being penalised.

Maddy said she could understand. As per the process, the L1 manager has to provide not just the score but also the justification for the score. As he had already observed the draft score he must have read through the draft comments as well, had he?

Jagan said that he hadn't. He was so upset looking at the score that he had called right away.

Maddy told him to go back, look at the comments and call back if he still believed that the score was not correct. This gave him and Maddy some time to recompose themselves. He, to reassess his belief and Maddy, to gather her thoughts.

Context: Maddy had followed up with Jagan and other team members on an exercise in capability building that they were undertaking at all their sites. This project involved drawing up a skill map of each unique role at the sites, both in terms of functional and behavioural skills. There were four layers, the doers / individual contributors (ICs), the two layers of supervisors/ managers and the last layer of function leaders / department heads. The board itself was setting and driving this agenda. The board wanted to know if they had the capability to execute the business asks. If not, where were the gaps? What was the plan to plug those gaps and finally the roadmap to come back to 'achievement of goals'. Everything depended on the assessment of skills of the existing workforce, the starting point.

And Maddy knew they were behind schedule on this task at Jagan's site as well as another of his colleague's. Maddy had given both of them this feedback in their monthly performance assessment. Maddy knew they would come back but this was sooner than she expected.

Soon enough, Jagan's call came. He seemed more upset this time. He had found that Maddy had given him positive feedback on all aspects of work except the progress on capability building. He vehemently protested the harsh rating based on only one lapse. He said, "I have completed all tasks as per expectation. You have given the feedback yourself. I have missed showing progress on this one task. You know I have kept you posted on the lack of progress. There's been an audit at the site. The site leadership was tied up the whole month in its preparation and then in facing the audit. I have escalated the delay to the site head. He had written a strong email to all his direct reports stating that this is a high priority, and they must accord it time. You were copied on that email. With all the efforts in front of you and the impossibility of progress in the face of audit taking priority, how can you penalise me for the same thing? This is unfair."

Jagan was a level-headed guy, but Maddy could hear the stress in his voice. She heard him take some water at the end of his monologue. He was hardly in the frame of mind to receive tough feedback. Maddy had to make a choice, give him the feedback straight as it is and let him face it or let things cool a bit and then take this up. Seconds were ticking. Maddy was in two minds.

Then Maddy asked herself, "If she cannot convince her team member of the rating and find a way for him to accept it willingly, how can she be sure she had done the right assessment? And if she had done a fair assessment and still couldn't pass a stress test of the system within HR, how did she expect others to be successful in using this system?" Maddy decided it had to be a 'use case'. She took the leap of faith and started.

Maddy said, "You are right, Jagan, we exchanged emails on this subject right up to the last day of the month. And speaking of emails, could you recall when was the first email on this subject?"

Jagan was struggling to recall. He was prepared for the current month's data. This was kind of out of context. Maddy helped him by asking him to look for an email from 3 months before. He took some time. They were on a call across different locations and on their respective laptops. In a few seconds his voice came back online, "Ya, I found it. But that was the introductory email. I have been following up on calls with the managers all these months without success. Even if the work was started 3 months ago, what is the reason for giving a '0' in this month?"

Maddy said, "Jagan, you referred to emails, so I referred

to emails that you had missed taking into consideration. If you wish to refer to speaking to people, fine, let us take this line of action. You will agree with me that we speak at least once every week (planned weekly catch-up). You would recall I had pulled you up on the lack of progress on this very subject in the middle of the month. Would you believe that you had your forewarning?"

Jagan wouldn't have any of it. He immediately shot back, "Yes you had, but I had informed that day as well that we will not be able to complete the task within timeline. Even then, you are penalizing me. It's not fair".

Maddy asked him, "Ok, so are we saying that we shouldn't be held responsible for our failures if we have announced them ahead of time? How does pre-announcement reduce the lack of results?"

Jagan said, "If you set a target that can't be achieved due to externalities like audit, giving prior information is like saying it in advance that the target setting is incorrect."

The conversation was becoming really interesting and challenging. It had reached a stage from where, depending on how it flowed, it would end in disaster or breakthrough. Maddy had to make that attempt. She said, "Jagan, you are right. There was no way you could have achieved this task this month. I accept. Now you have seen that we didn't start this task this month. We did so three months back. There was no progress on this task for the last two months. Did we discuss the lack of progress in those months?"

Jagan: Yes, we did.

Maddy: Did I give you a poor rating in the last two months despite the lack of progress there?

Jagan: No.

Maddy: Now how many months are left for us to complete this task?

Jagan: 2 more months remain in the year.

Maddy: I gave you verbal feedback during the last two months on the lack of progress and yet gave you 100% score in those months. Despite my "Good Samaritan" behaviour, you didn't take the feedback seriously. If you had, we wouldn't have come to the third month and faced external challenges. So, do you now have conclusive, hands-on experience that feedback without consequences falls on deaf ears? Free advice does not work. Do you also see that feedback accompanied by 'poor rating' has made you charged up and willing to challenge me? So, tell me, don't you have the clearest proof now that the psychological basis of the system is sound, and your current case is the live 'proof of the pudding'?

At this point, Jagan was silent for the longest time Maddy could remember. Finally, when he spoke, the stress and tension was gone. He was back to his calm and composed self. He spoke in a measured voice, "I see the merit of giving a rating and not just feedback. I accept the previous two months' feedback didn't hit as hard as the '0' this month. Okay, I admit I slipped. I slipped despite several chances at improvement. I admit this month was a non-starter, but I had previous months that were lean on work. I could have got this done beforehand. But now it's 'split milk'. No point in crying over it."

Maddy said, "No Jagan, we have discussed only one aspect of our system, i.e. feedback accompanied by a rating is far more effective than feedback alone. However, our system is not uni-dimensional. We also promise this is a windshield way of working rather than a rear-view mirror driving. So, there's a possibility."

Jagan: No, the rating is already given. I accept the feedback. But what's done it done. There's no turning the clock back.

Maddy: Wait! In the old way of working, the feedback was given after the year was over. It was a lose-lose proposition. You couldn't go back to the last year and mend it. The organisation couldn't do the same for the same reasons. Here, the year is not over. We have 2 more months. I gave you a '0' because I believed you will miss the year-end target. I gave you this feedback with 2 more months remaining. If you and your site head focus on this task alongside other deliverables, you can still complete it before the year ends, i.e. on time.

Jagan: Oh yes! But wait. How does that help? It may help the company achieve its annual target, but I have lost my score.

Maddy: Who said you have? If you are able to make up the lost time, you would work double hard to achieve it. And if you did achieve it, let's say you are back on track by end of next month, then I am forced to reassess my assumption that you will miss the target. Then I am perforce required to give you a '2' to recompense and recognise your recovery. In the process, the company achieves its goals, and you achieve yours. How's that for a win-win vis-a-vis the lose-lose of previous regime?

Jagan: Would you really give me a '2' next month?

Maddy: If you turn this around, I will be left with no choice. Besides, I would be achieving my year-end targets with your help. I would have every reason to make sure I pass the benefit on to you just like I am passing on my (expected) failure on to you. We succeed as a team or fail as a team. This is the other aspect of this system.

Jagan: I didn't realise how powerful this system is. I will get to work right away. Wish me luck. No wait. Wish me '2'.

And they both laughed as they closed the call.

THE BUTTERFLY EFFECT

Daniel was speaking with Maddy. He was the site head of the German facility. Maddy had gone to their German facility, and they were meeting over lunch. After some chitchat, Maddy congratulated him on the success of the internal audit and wished him luck for the external audit. The team must have put in a lot of effort. Once they pass the external audit, they will be eligible to export outside EU. This would boost their bottom line. Daniel (Dan) agreed. But what ensued was very interesting and unexpected for Maddy.

It went something like this: Dan had congratulated the team for completing their preparations for the external audit. The corporate internal audit team had come and pitched tent at the facility for a month in advance. They had reviewed each and every process element; the batch records, the deviations and the closure reports. Many gaps were found. This was not unusual. It was the job of internal audit to find gaps and address them before external auditor came looking for them.

The site team got down to work. Over the next few weeks, they had worked tirelessly towards completing the documentation and bringing the records up to date. This required change controls and signing off 'out of specification' (OOS) and 'out of trend' (OOT) observations. Some of them needed acceptance of errors done in the past, not a very pleasant admission. But the message was clear, the auditors would view an error and admission thereof more leniently than a cover up of errors. In quality management, you can strike off an incorrect data point, sign across it, write the correct data point next to it and it will be acceptable. Try erasing the earlier data point and overwrite the correct data on top, and that would be the surest way to get a warning letter from an auditor.

At the end of it, the internal audit gave the thumbs up to the site readiness. It was a relief for the site. And that's where Dan noticed something he would have ignored earlier.

The managers had given high performance scores to their team members for the hard work put in during the previous month. Many of the executives got the 'above expectation' performance rating. There was general back slapping going around. The site leadership, cognizant of the outcome orientation of the system, not efforts, had informed Dan that this month must be treated as a high outcome month.

Dan, for his part, would have considered the hard work done by the team and its stamp of approval given by the internal auditors as a positive outcome. Under the previous system, this would have been a feather in the cap of the team. But looking at month on month performance and outcome had shifted Daniel's paradigm, permanently. He asked his leadership two simple questions.

A. If the internal auditors had not come and the external auditors had found these gaps, what would the leadership have assessed their teams' performance as, 'above expectations', 'as per expectations', or 'below expectations'?

The response from the function leaders was a meek 'below expectations'. With so many gaps, the team had not done its regular job.

B. If the internal auditors identified the gaps and now the team has plugged the gaps, what would this work be assessed as?

Some function leaders now saw what Dan was driving at. They started nodding that the 'below expectations' had just become 'as per expectations'. After all, the team had only done what was expected of them. They were behind in terms of results. With the help of the internal audit team, they were able to come to par.

And this is where Dan took it a step further. He pointed out that compliance to procedure was a minimum expectation. There were no prizes for maintaining minimum expected standards like safety, regulatory compliance, statutory compliance, and an error free work environment. The team was in fact not compliant with the requirement before the internal audit. On that count itself, the entire team should have been given 'below expected' results and ratings for the previous months. It is a miracle that we don't have to face embarrassment in front of the external auditors (fingers crossed). Instead of pulling up the team for their past behaviour, the function leaders were praising them to the heavens and recommending a high-performance score for addressing their own previous failures!

The last sentence hurt the function leaders the most. Dan knew. There was pin drop silence for a moment. Dan spoke again in a softer tone. He exhorted his team to do a more careful assessment of their team in future. He was ready to accept 'at par performance' for those who had been erroneously given 'above par performance' if the function leaders revised their recommendations. But he would assess the function leaders' performance as 'below par performance' if they continued this kind of performance assessment of their team. The meeting had ended with no further talk.

Recalling this incident, Dan thanked Maddy and said, "Had it not been for the month-on-month assessment, I could not have spotted the gap in my own leadership team's assessment. I could not have brought the paradigm shift in them, had I not had the process to discuss the topic when it was hot and give a rating revision that would be accepted and remain in their memory. But most of all, none of us could have received the clarity with which we view performance today vis-à-vis previously. Most of what happened was unplanned, but it could not have happened without the anchor of the new performance management system, Maddy. So, thank you."

EPILOGUE
CHAMPION AMONG WINNERS

It was the April month and a year after the launch of the month-on-month performance management system. The performance scores for the year had come in. The HRIT team had downloaded the monthly scores and handed them over to HR. Maddy's team had summed up the monthly scores to arrive at the annual scores for the year. Maddy was looking at the data for the first time. A median score of 12 out of 12 would denote a 100% people performance or a 3 out of 5 score in the previous regime. It was 11 out of 12 (~92%) due to the business performance being 87%. The process had passed the first test. Then she checked the spread of scores. The lowest score was 8 and the highest score was 17 (out of 12). She noted that the worst case that would still pass muster was expected at three 0s, the highest tolerance level for an organization without individual performances dragging the aggregate down. A score of '8' meant four 0s, a consequence of 87% business performance. This needed further examination and action.

Anyway, what drew her attention even more was the other side. The high-performance side was expected to have three 2s leading to a high score of 15 (out of 12). This was indeed the case. The number of 16 scores were few (like the number of 8 scorers). However, one, just one employee had managed to score a 17 out of 12. That was five 2s in a round of 12 (with seven 1s). Maddy was curious to know more about this case. Who could score 2, five times out of 12 times. It must have taken a lot of positive results or a lot of luck or a lot of boss-pleasing to reach this level of score in such a stringent and frequent scoring process. Maddy had a hunch this was favouritism by the L1 manager that somehow had escaped the notice of the L2 manager and site leaders as well. This had to be brought down to a saner level. Maddy dug deeper. What she found would redefine her perception.

Akhilesh was a supervisor in engineering services. He had worked in two other reputed organizations before joining them three years ago. His first rating two years ago was a 5 on 5, the highest performer. Maddy knew the unwritten rule of team management, the new guys don't land a plum rating in the first year. That's reserved for the long-timers. The new guys have to work and prove themselves to earn that highest rating. So how did Akhilesh manage a '5 on 5' in the first year itself? Anyway, what was more surprising was that he had landed a '5 on 5' the next year as well. Maddy realised this was not a fluke. This guy was doing something right. Otherwise, he would have lost out on the next unwritten rule of the manager's game, rotate the best performer rating among the team; managers were known to allocate best performer rating on a round robin format. They would give this rating to someone in a year, recommend his/her promotion, then give the next best performer rating to another employee and recommend a compensation correction or some such thing. Basically, it was a gamified version of something for everyone. Managers were using the rating system to take care of their teams' aspirations, financial and social. The entire organization knew how this played out and played along to survive. Akhilesh seemed to break that pattern; rather he seemed to have forced his L1 manager to break the pattern.

Now with an out of world rating of 17 out of 12, he was being given a 142% performance assessment. And how were his colleagues not protesting this blatant favouritism? What was going on! The more Maddy studied the data, the more confused it made her. She decided to call the function leader at the site, Girish.

Girish was genuinely pleased to have received a call from the Head of HR. After the general chit-chat Maddy asked what he knew about Akhilesh. She was surprised when Girish said, he expected to be asked about Akhilesh sooner rather than later; just that he didn't expect it to come directly from Maddy, herself. Nonetheless, he was prepared.

Akhilesh came in three years back when the site engineering was struggling with instrument breakdowns. They site was old, instruments equally old and breakdown was expected; not with Akhilesh. He called up the instrument validation team and checked the next preventive maintenance timetable. Accordingly, he prepared a risk assessment matrix, the later the maintenance check, the higher the risk. He worked with his L1 manager and Girish, his L2 manager to advance the AMC maintenance visit wherever there was more time for the validation group to come and inspect. This way all the instruments were either checked by the inhouse validation group or the external AMC provider within two months. After this thorough overhaul, the breakdowns came down proportionally. There was a great deal of savings to the organization due to this innovative thinking of Akhilesh. This was how he had earned his spurs in the first year. Maddy understood now, this was no exception.

More innovative thinking and execution from Akhilesh followed next year earning Akhilesh another 5 out of 5. And during this round, his L1 manager had told Girish that 5 out of 5 was actually insufficient to acknowledge the superior contribution Akhilesh was bringing to the team. He had asked if they could recommend a special bonus or a promotion or something. Girish had shot down the promotion idea saying Akhilesh should be rewarded for his performance. If he is to be promoted, that should be done considering his potential to do the next level job. This and that should not be mixed. Anyway, it was left at that.

The introduction of the new performance management system, Girish said to Maddy, was in fact a solution for higher performers among the high performers, like Akhilesh. The previous system did not have much option to provide micro-level details of this sort. With the launch of the new system, Girish and his team were able to differentiate Akhilesh's performance without having to reduce the other high performers' ratings just to ensure high visibility for Akhilesh. Both he and other high performers had their place in the sun in this new system.

Girish and Maddy closed the call with pleasantries. Long afterwards, Maddy kept on thinking, about what positive forces had the system released without her actively planning! She realised systems have their own way of spawning their own outcomes. Much like AI, once released, systems have a life of their own. All the more reason, she should ensure she implemented systems and processes with potential net positive impact.

---x---

ACKNOWLEDGEMENT

Thank you, my family, for supporting me throughout this journey, with its crests and troughs, bearing with the inconveniences, celebrating the successes, and making the experience memorable.

Thank you, Prabir Jha, Atul Dhavle, Sridhar VVS, Narayan Reddy V, Ram Mohan Chepuri, Kaushik Mitter, Sourav Mohapatra, Rajorshi Ganguli, Dinesh Chandra Kandwal, Sandip Mishra, Rahul Mukherjee, and Sanjay Jog. I had the fortune of working with you, see you work, and learn from you.

Thank you, Neeraj Sharma, Sundhar CK, Biju Mathew, Swamy KN, and Prateek Gupta. Without your support and encouragement, this concept would not have been implemented at the size and scale it did. Thank you, Chidanand Vasanth, Sashikala R, Agnieszka Sadzikowska, Anna Gembarowska, Shailendra Sharma, Ranjana S, Kiran Kumar S, Vijaykumar HR, Deepak Ghosh, Rashmi Kumari and team for keeping the faith through the formative stages.

Thank you, my business colleagues, my team, my friends, and my fellow travellers, for joining in the experiments, walking through the rough and tumble, shaping the concept with your feedback, partaking in the benefits, and forgiving the missteps that inevitably accompany an experiment of this size and scale. We have run this system with a cumulative 4000+ employees, generating 30000+ unique employee-wise monthly performance scores, given by 300+ managers over 36 months. I hope we all enjoyed the fruits of our labour.

Thank you 'Darwinbox' team for partnering in the journey, configuring and running the digital customizations that enabled the system to churn out of large-scale datasets, thus providing the proof of the concept.

Thank you Sweta Samota, my book coach.

Special thanks to Akhilesh Singh, a man I have never met nor seen, only spoken with during my Reliance Jio days – for seeding the thought with 'Mishra ji, you should write a book'. Thank you, Akhilesh ji.

ABOUT THE AUTHOR

Murari Madhab Mishra (Triple M) is an MA (Psychology), an MBA (XIMB), and an MS (Chemistry). He has about 20 years of experience working in pharmaceutical, energy and digital technology sectors. 'Triple M' has worked with organizations like Dr. Reddy's, Reliance Jio, Steriscience/OneSource apart from an entrepreneurial stint with his start-up. He has extensive domain expertise in performance management, organization design, talent management, and business partnering. He has worked in and for markets in Asia, Europe & the Americas. He has designed the 'new' performance management system and successfully implemented it in the organizations he has worked for. He is a polyglot and nurtures diverse hobbies in individual and team sports.

For more information, please visit: www.mmmishra.com or www.linkedin.com/in/murari-madhab-mishra-triple-m-5402ba1

www.ingramcontent.com/pod-product-compliance
Lightning Source LLC
Chambersburg PA
CBHW071534220526
45469CB00003B/769